NICE
THE FRENCH RIVIERA
MADE EASY

Andy Herbach

Europe Made Easy
Travel Guides

Europe Made Easy
Travel Guides

www.eatndrink.com

NICE AND THE FRENCH RIVIERA MADE EASY
ISBN: 9798806435096
–All Rights Reserved–
Third Edition 2022
Andy Herbach

Acknowledgments
Contributor: Karl Raaum
All photos from Shutterstock, Pixabay, and Karl Raaum
Editor: Marian Modesta Olson

ABOUT THE AUTHOR
Andy Herbach is the author of the *Eating & Drinking* series
of menu translators and restaurant guides, including *Eating
& Drinking in Paris, Eating & Drinking in Italy, Eating &
Drinking in Spain and Portugal,* and *Eating & Drinking in Latin
America.* He is also the author of several travel guides, including
*Paris Walks, The Next Time I See Paris, Europe Made Easy, Paris
Made Easy, Amsterdam Made Easy, Berlin Made Easy, Barcelona
Made Easy, Madrid Made Easy, Oslo Made Easy, Provence Made
Easy, Palm Springs Made Easy, The Amazing California Desert,*
and *San Diego Made Easy.*

Andy is a lawyer and resides in Palm Springs, California.

You can e-mail corrections, additions, and comments to
eatndrink@aol.com or through
www.eatndrink.com.

∽

TABLE OF CONTENTS

MAPS

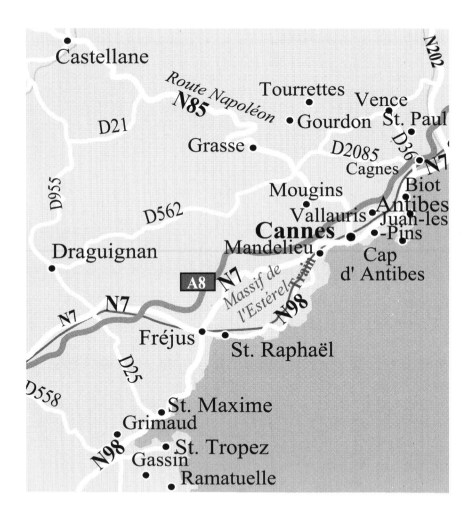

**French Riviera
(Côte d'Azur)**

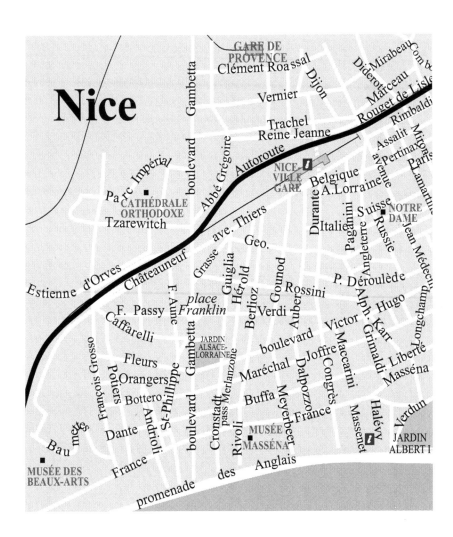

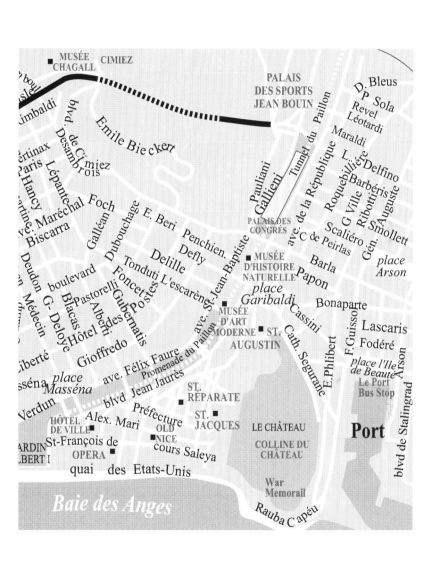

1. INTRODUCTION

On the **French Riviera**, you'll discover pastel-colored villas with red tile roofs looking down on the turquoise waters of the Mediterranean Sea.

Some come for the savory cuisine and wonderful wines, while others visit quiet villages to get away from it all. There are also some of the world's best-preserved Roman ruins to see, and elegant seaside resorts where you can bask on sun-drenched beaches. You'll be dazzled by fields of lavender, yellow sunflowers, and bright red poppies under brilliant blue skies.

Whatever your reasons to visit, there's truly something for everyone on the French Riviera. Wherever you go, you'll create colorful memories.

You'll have over 100 places of interest at your fingertips, with tips on cafes, restaurants, hotels, shops, outdoor markets, and where to sample great wines.

This guide covers all the information you need to plan your trip without burdening you with a long list of options that simply aren't worth your precious vacation time. Forget those large, bulky travel books. This handy little guide is all you need to make your visit enjoyable, memorable–and *easy!*

2. OVERVIEW

Get ready to explore Roman ruins, eat fantastic food, enjoy bustling outdoor markets, or just sit in the sun and sip a glass of chilled wine.

Nice
Nice has on average 300 sunny days a year, many important historical sights and museums, a fabulous Old Town, and great dining.

The Eastern French Riviera: From Nice to the Italian Border
The French lifestyle with an Italian feel greets you in this part of the French Riviera. Some of the highlights here include the lovely hillop Eze, upscale St-Jean-Cap-Ferrat, and the quaint harbor town of Villefranche-sur-Mer. We'll also visit swanky Monaco.

The Western French Riviera: From St-Tropez to Nice
Hilltop villages, art museums, coastal resorts and a St-Tropez tan all await you in the western French Riviera. You'll also visit picturesque villages and great beaches in places like Grimaud, Antibes, and Cannes.

3. NICE

HIGHLIGHTS

- Strolling on the Promenade des Anglais

- Wandering Nice's Old Town (Vieux Nice)

- Chagall paintings at the Musée National Message Biblique

- Avant-garde art at the Musée d'Art Moderne et d'Art Contemporain

- People-watching and dining on the colorful cours Saleya

Nice (population 350,000) is in the south of France on the Mediterranean Sea, just 25 miles (40km) from the Italian border. It's 20 miles (33km) northeast of Cannes and 567 miles (912km) south of Paris.

For most travelers, Nice is the introduction to the fabulous French Riviera. Nice's airport is the second busiest in France (after Paris). Why some avoid the city is perplexing. Nice, on the Baie des Anges (Bay of Angels), has on average 300 sunny days a year, many important historical sights and museums, a fabulous Old Town, and great dining.

Nice was part of Italy until 1860 and you'll see the Italian influence in everything from architecture to cuisine. Yes, it's a large city, but if you simply take time to experience it, you'll learn to love Nice.

The **Nice-Côte d'Azur Airport** is on a peninsula 20 minutes west of the central city of Nice. A taxi into town costs at least €32. Rideshare to central Nice costs around €20.

Trams run seven days a week from 5am until midnight. On weekdays, trams run every five minutes from 7:30am to 8:00pm. On Saturdays, trams arrive every six minutes between 7:00am and 8:00pm. Sunday trams run every nine minutes between 8:00am and 9:00pm. For €1.50, a single pass has unlimited transfers on buses or trams within 74 minutes of validation (one direction only). Bus tickets may be purchased from the driver, but tram tickets must be purchased before boarding at vending machines at the stop. The machines only take credit cards with chips or Euro coins. A 10-ride pass cost €10 (€1 per ride) and may be used by more than one person on the same trip.

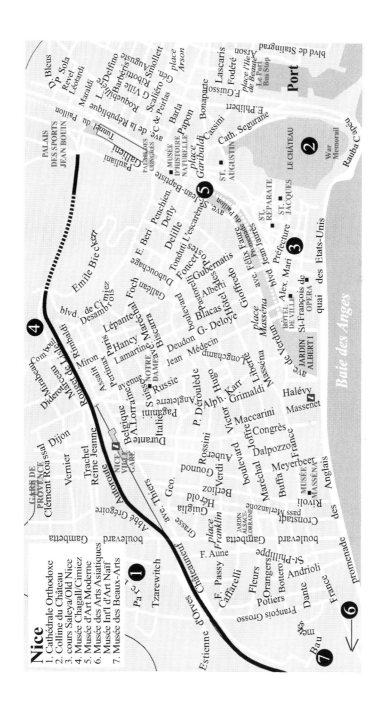

Nice
1. Cathédrale Orthodoxe
2. Colline du Château
3. cours Saleya/Old Nice
4. Musée Chagall/Cimiez
5. Musée d'Art Moderne
6. Musée des Arts Asiatiques
7. Musée Int'l d'Art Naïf
7. Musée des Beaux-Arts

Port

Baie des Anges

NICE SIGHTS

Promenade des Anglais
This wide boulevard runs four miles along the entire length of Nice's waterfront. The name means "walkway of the English" because it was financed by wealthy English tourists who came here in droves in the 1800s in search of sun and sea. Today it's a beautiful walk made all the more interesting by sunbathers, walkers, runners, and skaters from so many different parts of the world. Oh, and put your eyes back into your head. While nudity is prohibited, topless bathing is not. The beaches here are made up of large uncomfortable rocks. At the east end of the promenade it becomes the quai des Etats-Unis. You can head to any number of beach clubs along the promenade. For around €20, you'll get a chair and cushion and waiter service while you relax in the sun. We like Hi-Beach and Castel Plage. Be warned that waiter service here can be (shall we say) leisurely!

The main **tourist information center** is located at 2 promenade des Anglais. Tel. 08/92.70.74.07. Open daily 9am-6pm (until 7pm in summer). There are also branches at the airport and main train station. www.nicetourism.com.

Jardin Albert-1er
The Albert I Garden is a public park that links the Promenade des Anglais with Vieux Nice (Old Town). Developed in the 1800s, you'll find locals and tourists relaxing surrounded by exotic palms and flowers. *Info: avenue de Verdun/avenue des Phocéens. Open daily. Free.*

Cours Saleya

This has been the main street of Vieux Nice (Old Town) since the Middle Ages. You must come here if you visit Nice. At times it seems that everyone in Nice is here, especially at night when its restaurants and cafés fill with locals and tourists. It's the home to a wonderful daily flower and food market. On Mondays, it's an antique market. Walk through the maze of narrow streets in Old Nice past small churches and under drying laundry for photo opportunities at every turn.

Hôtel Negresco

Prominently located on the promenade des Anglais, this hotel is a Nice landmark. Even if you don't dine or drink here, step inside and admire this incredible building. From the lobby, you can visit the Salon Royal with its immense 19th-century Baccarat crystal chandelier and dome. *Info: 37 promenade des Anglais.*

Place Masséna

This beautiful square is named after Jean-André Masséna, one of France's great military heroes. You might feel like you're in Italy rather than France with its rococo buildings. The place is elegant with black-and-white pavement and bubbling fountains. The modern art addition features lit men on pedestals high above you. You'll find shopping for all budgets around the square. *Photo on next page.*

Promenade du Paillon

This green parkway connects the Jardin Albert-1er with the MAMAC (modern art museum). Filled with palm trees and exotic Mediterranean plants, this is a wonderful addition to Nice's central city.

Musée Masséna

This Belle Époque beachfront villa is filled with paintings from French, Italian, and Dutch masters. We especially liked the exhibit of images of Nice throughout the years. Don't miss the lovely garden. *Info: 35 promenade des Anglais/65 rue de France. www. massena-nice.org. Tel. 04/93.91.19.10. Open Wed-Mon 10am-6pm in summer (11am-6pm in Winter). Closed Tue. Admission: €15.*

Place Rossetti/Cathédrale Ste-Réparate

This elegant square is another example of Nice's connection to Italy. Look around and you might feel as if you're in Milan or Rome instead of in France. On the square is Nice's cathedral. It's another wonderful example of Baroque architecture with intricate plasterwork and elaborate frescoes. The cathedral is named after the patron saint of Nice. She was a teenage virgin whose martyred body is said to have floated to Nice in the 4th century accompanied by angels (really?). This is how the city's Baie des Anges (Bay of Angels) got its name. *Info: place Rossetti. Cathedral closed noon-2pm (Mon-Sat) and 1pm-3pm (Sun). Admission: Free. www.cathedrale-nice.fr.*

Musée des Beaux-Arts Jules-Chéret (Jules-Chéret Fine Arts Museum)
Housed in a 19th-century mansion, this museum on the west side of town, contains works of former residents of the city (including those of the man from whom the museum takes its name). Artists on display include Monet, Degas, Sisley, Dufy, Bonnard, and Renoir. There are also ceramic works by Picasso, and sculpture by Rodin. *Info: 33 avenue des Baumettes. Tel. 04/92.15.28.28. Open Tue-Sun 10am-6pm (Nov-Apr 11am-6pm). Closed Mon. Admission: €10. www.musee-beaux-arts-nice.org.*

Musée d'Art Moderne et d'Art Contemporain
You can't miss the contemporary structures (four gray marble towers) that house this museum of avant-garde art from the 1960s to today. Works featured here include those by Lichtenstein and Warhol. Check out the fantastic rooftop terrace. *Info: promenade des Arts/place Yves Klein. Tel. 04/97.13.42.01. Open Tue-Sun 10am-6pm. (Nov-Apr 11am-6pm). Closed Mon. Admission: €10. www.mamac-nice.org.*

Colline du Château
High on a rock above the city are the ruins of a castle that was destroyed in 1706. The ruins are now a park and gardens. You have fantastic views of the foothills of the Alps, the bay, the waterfront promenade, and the red-tile roofs of Old Nice. You can take an elevator to the top of this hill for free. The elevator is on the quai des Etats-Unis just to the left of the Hôtel Suisse. Elevator operates daily from 10am-7pm (until 8pm in summer). *Info: Colline du Château. Open daily. Admission: Free.*

Cathédrale Orthodoxe Russe St-Nicolas (Russian Orthodox Cathedral)
You'll know when you're getting close to this cathedral, as you can't help but notice its onion-shaped domes, so out of place on the Riviera. In 1912, Czar Nicholas II gave the cathedral to the large Russian community who lived and vacationed here. You'll feel like you're in Russia (or at least not in Nice) when you step

into its interior, filled with icons and incense. *Info: avenue Nicolas-II at 17 boulevard du Tzaréwitch. Tel. 09/81.09.53.45. Open daily 9am-noon and 2pm-6pm. Guided tours sometimes available for €10. www.sobor.fr.*

Musée des Arts Asiatiques
You'll find Asian paintings, sculpture, carvings and ceramics at this museum. It's housed in a sleek modern building built on an artificial lake in the 17-acre Parc Phoenix, a botanical garden. *Info: 405 promenade des Anglais. Tel. 04/89.04.55.20. Open Wed-Mon 10am-5pm (July and Aug until 6pm). Closed Tue. Admission: Free. English audioguide €2. www.arts-asiatiques.com.*

Musée International d'Art Naïf Anatole-Jakovsky
This museum is named after an art critic, and houses his collection of over 600 works of naïve art. You'll find everything from primitive paintings to American folk art here. *Info:* avenue de Fabron (in the Château St-Héléne). Tel. 04/93.71.78.33. Open Wed-Mon 10:30am-12:30pm and 1:30pm-6pm. Closed Tue. Admission: €10.

Cimiez
This hilltop neighborhood is located in the northeast part of town. The easiest way to get here (it's about three miles north of Old Nice) is to take bus number 5 from behind Galeries Lafayette (Masséna/Guitry stop). Get off at the Musée Chagall stop.

You'll find the Parc des Antiquités at the top of the hill. This former arena and its gardens contain Roman ruins dating back to the first century.

Cimiez is home to two museums by famous artists with connections to this city.

Musée National Message Biblique–Marc Chagall

Russian painter Marc Chagall (who later became a French citizen) donated the collection at this museum to France, and it's among the largest anywhere. He was often influenced by religious themes, and you'll find his "Biblical Message" on display here. These 12 large paintings illustrate the first two books of the Old Testament. The museum has lovely gardens filled with herbs, olive trees, and pools. *Info: avenue du Dr-Ménard (in Cimiez). Tel. 04/93.53.87.20. Open Wed-Mon May-Oct 10am-6pm (Nov-Apr until 5pm). Closed Tue. Admission: €10. Buses #5 and the Nice-Le Grand Tour Bus stop at the museum (Musée Chagall stop). www.musee-chagall.fr.*

Musée Matisse

The Matisse Museum, located in a 17th-century villa, contains the largest collection of paintings by Henri Matisse, who spent the last years of his life in Nice, and some of his personal effects are on display.

Matisse is one of the 20th century's greatest painters. Most of his works here were created while he resided in Nice. Everything from his works as a student to his late-life works–from nudes to religious art–is featured here. Among the famous works are his *Blue Nude IV* and *Nude in Armchair with a Green Plant. Info: 164 avenue des Arènes-de-Cimiez (in Cimiez). Tel. 04/93.81.08.08. Open Wed-Mon 10am-6pm. Closed Tue. Admission: €10, under 18 free. Bus #5 stops at the museum (Arènes/Musée Matisse stop). musee-matisee-nice.org.*

Musée Franciscain/Église et Monastère de Cimiez

This sight in Cimiez also has a Matisse connection. This Franciscan monastery is still home to monks. There are lovely gardens with panoramic views (Matisse is buried in the cemetery), a museum dedicated to the history of the Franciscan order, and a 15th-century church with elegant works by Bréa. *Info: place du Monastère (in Cimiez). Tel. 04/93.81.08.08. Museum open Mon-Sat 10am-noon and 3pm-5:30pm. Closed Sun. Admission: Free.*

Musée Archéologique

This archeology museum is filled with Roman finds from the Cimiez area. *Info: 160 avenue des Arènes-de-Cimiez (in Cimiez). Tel. 04/93.81.59.57. Open Wed-Mon 10am-6pm (Nov-Apr until 5pm). Closed Tue. Admission: €5. www.musee-archeologie-nice.org.*

The Beaches East of the Port and the Sentier de Mer

One of our favorite places in Nice is an area often ignored by travelers. Past the port (to the east) you'll find boulevard Franck Pilatte. Follow this boulevard along the sea. Look for the signs "Sentier de Mer." This is a walkway that runs along the sea. There are several small and rocky beaches in this area and restaurants and bars with great views of the city. The path ends at Coco Beach.

Museum Pass

You can purchase a €20 seven-day pass for entry to 14 museums. A 24-hour pass costs €10. Participating museums include Musée Matisse, the Modern and Contemporary Art Museum, Fine Arts Museum, Archaeological Museum, Palais Lascaris, and Masséna Museum.

A Walk in Nice's Old Town

Begin your walk at the **Jardin Albert-1er** on the **promenade des Anglais** between avenue de Verdun and boulevard Jean-Jaurès.

Take in the sunbathers, runners and other walkers on the promenade des Anglais, the waterfront boulevard. Along the promenade is the **Jardin Albert 1er** (Albert I Garden). It's filled with exotic palms and flowers. Here, the promenade becomes the **quai des Etats-Unis.**

As you're heading toward the giant rock, turn left onto **avenue des Phocéens** and take the first right onto **rue St-François-de-Paule.**

You're now in Nice's **Old Town** (Vieux Nice). At number 14 (on your right) is **Alziari**, the place for fragrant olive oil (for sale in many sizes of blue and yellow tins), olive soap, and olive spread. On your left at number 9 is the beautiful **Eglise St-François-de-Paule** (also called Eglise des Dominicains), the sight of frequent classical concerts. Step inside and admire its beautiful interior. At number 7 (on your left) is the picturesque storefront of **Confiserie Auer.** This candy shop has been in business since 1820 and counts Queen Victoria as one of its famous customers.

At number 4 (on the right) is the opulent **Opéra de Nice.** The four statues on top represent singing, music, dance, and theatre, and

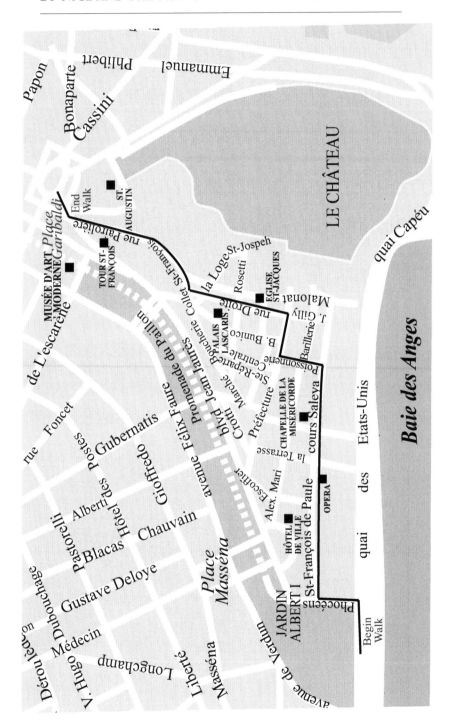

the opera house is home to Nice's chorus, orchestra, opera, and ballet. Charles Garnier, the designer of this building, also created the famous opera house in Paris and the casino in Monte Carlo.

Notice the bilingual street signs are in French and the old Niçois language (an Italian dialect).

Continue down rue St-François-de-Paule to the cours Saleya.

To your left is the **Palais des Ducs de Savoie** (Dukes of Savoy Palace), parts of which date back to 1559. This was the home of the kings of Sardinia, Nice's Italian rulers until 1860. It's now the police headquarters.

The colorful **cours Saleya** is the main street of Old Nice and has been since the Middle Ages. It's home to a wonderful daily flower and food market. On Mondays, it's an antiques market. Relax at one of the many cafés that line the street.

On your left on the cours Saleya is the **Chapelle de la Miséricorde**. Stop in and take in the chapel's splendor. Filled with chandeliers, faux marble, frescoes, and carved wood, it's one of the world's best examples of the Baroque style. *Info: cours Saleya. Open daily. Admission: Free.*

See that yellow stone building at the end of cours Saleya? Artist **Henri Matisse** lived there from 1921 to 1938.

Before leaving the cours Saleya, sample *socca*, a crêpe made with chickpea flour. There are several places that serve *socca*.

Many of the restaurants here also serve the specialty *pissaladière*, a pizza-like tart with onions, black olives and purée of anchovies and sardines.

Turn left at **rue de la Poissonnière.**

On this small street is **Eglise Notre-Dame de l'Annonciation** (on your left). Check out the church's elaborate interior. This Baroque church is dedicated to St. Rita, the patron of desperate causes (does she know some of our friends?). Notice the interesting chapel on the right featuring St. Erasmus, the protector of mariners. *Info: 1 rue de la Poissonerie. Open daily. Admission: Free.*

Turn right onto rue de la Préfecture and then left onto rue Droite.

At the intersection of rue Droite and place du Jésus is **Eglise du Jésus** (Gesu). Stop in if you haven't seen enough churches. The plain exterior doesn't prepare you for the incredible over-the-top Baroque interior. Notice the wooden pulpit and the carved crucifix extending from it. *Info: Open daily. Admission: Free.*

At 15 rue Droite (on your left) is the sumptuous **Palais Lascaris,** built in the 17th century. There are 15 palaces in Old Town and this is the best and only one open to the public.

The palace is filled with tapestries and statues, and has one of the grandest staircases you'll ever see. *Info: 15 rue Droite. Tel. 04/93.62.72.40. Open Wed-Mon 10am-6pm. Closed Tue. Admission: €10.*

Continue on rue Droite until it ends and turn right onto rue St-François which turns into rue Pairolière.

You'll pass the **Tour St-François** (Tower of St. Francis), built in the 13th century, on your left at the square Jardin Auguste Icarte.

Continue down rue Pairolière.

The large square that you enter is **Place Garibaldi** (at rue Cassini). This very Italian-looking square was created at the end of the 18th century. In the center stands a statue and fountain of Joseph Garibaldi, an Italian patriot. You can end your walk here at one of the cafés.

Train Touristique

If you don't want to walk to the sights of Nice, try the rubber-wheeled **tourist train** (Train Touristique de Nice). It departs every 30 minutes from the Jardin Albert-1er (Albert I Garden) near the waterfront. The stop is located on the promenade des Anglais and avenue de Verdum. The trip takes 45 minutes and passes many of Nice's main sights and costs €10 (€5 ages 4-12). Who cares if you look like a dork? *Info: Tel. 06/08.55.03.30. Operates daily 10am to 5pm (extended hours in summer). www.francevoguette.com/trains-touristiques-a-nice.*

Sleeping in Nice

€€€ Expensive: Over €200
€€ Moderate: €100-€200
€ Inexpensive: Under €100
Double occupancy

Hôtel Negresco €€€

The grand dame of Nice hotels. Located on the promenade des Anglais, this luxurious hotel will pamper you in style. It's home to the Salon Royal with its immense 19th-century Baccarat crystal chandelier and dome. Le Chantecler, Nice's most prestigious restaurant, is also located here. *Info: 37 promenade des Anglais. Tel. 04/93.16.64.00 (hotel) 04/93.16.64.10 (restaurant). V, MC, DC, AE. Restaurants, bar, gym, AC, TV, telephone, minibar, hairdryer, WiFi. www.hotel-negresco-nice.com.*

Hyatt Regency Palais de la Méditerranée €€€

This Art Deco building has been renovated and offers fantastic views of the sea from its prime location on the Promenade des Anglais (Nice's seafront street and walkway), near Old Nice. Great outdoor pool. Its restaurant, Le 3e, serves Mediterranean cuisine on the poolside terrace. *Info: 13 Promenade des Anglais. Tel. 04/93.27.12.34 (hotel)/04/92.14.76.00 (restaurant). V, MC, AE. Restaurant, bar, outdoor pool, AC, TV, telephone, minibar, in-room safe, hairdryer, WiFi. www.lepalaisdelamediterranee.com.*

La Perouse €€€
This charming hotel is tucked into the hillside below the *château*, just a short walk from Old Nice. Great location, helpful staff, and a lovely pool. *Info: 11 quai Rauba-Capeau. Tel. 04/93.62.34.63. V, MC, DC, AE. Restaurant, bar, outdoor pool, TV, telephone, minibar, hairdryer, safe, WiFi. www.hotel-la-perouse.com.*

Hôtel Gounod €€
Built in the early 1900s, this 45-room hotel is a good, moderately priced choice in Nice's central city. It's about a five-minute walk to the beach. Comfortable and quiet guest rooms, and an added bonus is that guests can use the pool at the Hôtel Splendid next door. *Info: 3 rue Gounod. Tel. 04/93.16.42.00. V, MC, DC, AE. Restaurant, bar, gym, AC, TV, telephone, minibar, hairdryer, WiFi. www.gounod-nice.fr.*

Hôtel de la Fontaine €€
Located just off the promenade des Anglais and the beach, this 29-room hotel is on one of Nice's main shopping streets. The hotel was recently refurbished and features anti-allergy flooring, blankets, and pillows. Friendly staff. *Info: 49 rue de France. Tel. 04/93.88.30.38. V, MC, AE. AC, TV, telephone, hairdryer, safe, WiFi. www.hotel-fontaine.com.*

Ibis Styles Nice Centre Gare €€
This modern hotel has 135 air-conditioned and soundproof rooms. It's centrally located between the train station and the beaches. Standard rooms all have private bathrooms. Breakfast and WiFi are included. Parking is available (extra charge) at the nearby public Mozart car park. *Info: 3-5 Avenue Durante. Tel. 04/93.16.64.10. AC, TV, hairdryer, business center, free WiFi. www.accorhotels.com.*

Villa Saint-Exupéry (Beach) €
Budget travelers can stay in either basic rooms or dormitory communal rooms. It's a short walk from place Masséna and an easy walk to the beach. There's a gym, sauna, and bar. The hostel also organizes events and excursions. *Info: 6 rue Sacha Guitry. Tel. 04/93.16.13.45. V, MC. WiFi, gym, bar, lockers in rooms. www.villahostels.com.*

Riviera Pebbles (Apartments) €-€€€
One great way to truly experience life in the French Riviera is to rent an apartment. They're usually less expensive and larger than a hotel room. If we didn't have to check out hotels, we would always stay in an apartment. Many come with a washer/dryer combination that allows you to pack less. There are many apartments for rent through agencies such as Riviera Pebbles. *Info*: *www.rivierapebbles.com.*

Eating & Drinking in Nice

€€€€ Very Expensive: Over €30
€€€ Expensive: €21-€30
€€ Moderate: €11-€20
€ Inexpensive: Under €10
Prices are for a main course and without alcohol.
Credit cards accepted unless noted.

Le Chantecler €€€
Nice's most prestigious restaurant located in the luxurious Hôtel Negresco. It features such innovative dishes as crab-and-mango cannelloni. *Info: 37 promenade des Anglais. Tel. 04/93.16.64.10. Open Wed-Sun (dinner only). Closed Mon and Tue. Reservations required. www.hotel-negresco-nice.com.*

La Route du Miam €€-€€€
Rave reviews for this small restaurant located in a neighborhood north of the train station. You'll dine on specialties of southwest France in an intimate dining room. Staff is friendly and the wine list features wine from small producers. Try the sirloin steak served with *foie gras*. Also known for their duck (*canard*) dishes. Portions are generous. *Info: 1 rue Molière. Tel. 06/16.36.33.22. Closed Sun, Mon, and Tue (dinner only).*

La Merenda €€-€€€

This tiny bistro, run by the former chef at the Hôtel Negresco, has no phone. You have to stop by to make reservations in person, but it's worth it. Innovative cuisine, fresh ingredients and attentive service. *Info: 4 rue Raoul Bosio (formeryl rue de la Terrasse). No phone. No credit cards. Closed weekends, part of Aug, and two weeks at Christmas and New Year's. www.lamerenda.net.*

Le Tire Bouchon €€-€€€

This tiny bistro in the Old Town serves the specialties of the South of France. The *cassoulet* (a meat, bean and sausage casserole) is fantastic as is *la souris d'agneau braisée* (lamb shank served in a thyme sauce). Comfortable outdoor seating on the pedestrian street is also available. *Info: 19 rue de la Préfecture. Tel. 04/93.92.63.64. Closed Tue and Wed. le-tire-bouchon.com.*

La Part des Anges €-€€

Organic and biodynamic wines are gaining in popularity worldwide, and especially in France. This small wine shop and wine bar has a good selection of organic wines that you can down with *charcuterie* or cheese plates. There's also a small selection of hot dishes (the house specialty is pasta with razor clams). *Info: 17 rue Gubernatis (in the New Town off of rue Pastorelli). Tel 04/93.62.69.80. Open Mon-Sat 10am-8pm. Closed Sun. lapartdesanges-nice.com.*

Le Safari €€

Dine on Provençal and Niçoise specialties at this popular restaurant overlooking the flower market. We have eaten here frequently and the people-watching is great. The *gnocchi du jour* is always a good choice as is the *daube à la niçoise* (beef stew with red wine, tomatoes, and onions). This is the best of the touristy restaurants along the cours Saleya. *Info: 1 cours Saleya. Tel. 04/93.80.18.44. Open daily for lunch and dinner. www.restaurantsafari.fr.*

Pasta Basta €-€€

Good, hearty pasta dishes and pizza (and not a bad house wine either). *Info: 18 rue de la Préfecture. Tel. 04/93.80.03.57. Closed Thu. pastabasta.fr.*

Il Vicoletto €€

This Italian restaurant is located one block inland from the promenade des Anglais and near the Musée Masséna. You can dine outside along the pedestrian street or in the cozy restaurant. Try the *ravioli farciti verdure al burro e salvia* (ravioli stuffed with vegetables in a butter and sage sauce) or the garlicky *linguine alle vongole* (linguine with clams in a white wine sauce). The real deal here is the decent Italian house wine. *Info: 6 bis. Rue de France. Tel. 06/59.39.10.19. Closed Sun lunch. il-vicoletto.fr.*

La Rossettisserie €-€€

A rotisserie grill where you can watch your beef, chicken, pork, duck, veal, or lamb being cooked on the spit. Each meal is served with a choice of baked potatoes, mashed potatoes, or vegetable ratatouille. Located in Old Town near place Rossetti. Noisy and fun. *Info: 8 rue Mascoïnat. Tel. 04/93.76.18.80. Open Mon-Sat for lunch and dinner. Closed Sun. www.larossettisserie.com.*

La Cucina Nice €€-€€€

We love this small restaurant near Jardin Albert 1er. The eateries in this neighborhood are filled with a mixture of locals and tourists and this area is a suitable alternative to the more touristy restaurants along the cours Saleya. Friendly waiters serve both French and Italian dishes. Good Provençal wine list and delicious dishes such as duck, pasta arrabiatta, and creamy mushroom ravioli. *Info: 9 rue Commandant Raffalli. Tel. 09/83.48.91.39. Open daily for lunch and dinner. www.facebook.com/lacucina.nice.*

La Réserve €€€

If you're going to splurge for dinner in Nice, this is a good choice. This restaurant is located east of the Port de Nice. It offers stunning panoramic views of the Bay of Angels from its unique location with terraces overlooking the sea. The chef serves sophisticated and innovative cuisine. You'll love dining at this Art Deco restaurant. Truly an experience. Opt for La Grande Reserve menu at €79. *Info: 60 blvd Franck Pilatte. Tel. 04/97.08.14.80. Open daily for lunch and dinner. Closed Sun and Mon. www.lareservedenice.fr.*

Glacier Fenocchio

Try some of the best ice cream in the world. This family-owned institution has two locations in Old Nice. The main shop is at 2 place Rossetti facing the Cathédrale de Ste-Réparate. A second shop is just off the cours Saleya at 6 rue de la Poissonerie. Be adventurous and try one of the unique flavors like lavender, tomato, jasmin, or *comté de nice* (studded with pine nuts and candied mandarin). *Info: Tel. 04/93.80.72.52 (place Rossetti)/04/93.62.88.80 (rue de la Poissonerie). Open 9am to midnight. Poissonerie location closed Tue.*

Shopping in Nice

La Promenade des 100 Antiquaires

There are many antique shops on rue Catherine Ségurane and rue Emmanuel Philibert. Les Puces de Nice has 30 stalls under one roof on Quai Lunel (on Port de Nice). On each third Saturday of the month, there's an antique market on place Garibaldi. *Info: Closed Sun.*

Galeries Lafayette

This upscale department store has a wonderful food court in the basement and a restaurant on the fourth floor. *Info: 6 avenue Jean Médelin (near place Masséna). Tel. 04/92.17.36.36. Open daily 10am-8pm (Sun 11am-8pm). www.galerieslafayette.com.*

Confiserie Henri-Auer

This fantastic candy and chocolate shop near the opera house has been in business since 1820. *Info: 7 rue St-François-de-Paule. Tel. 04/93.85.77.98. Closed Sun. www.maison-auer.com.*

The colorful **cours Saleya** (the main street of Old Nice) has a wonderful daily flower and food market. On Mondays, it's an antiques market.

If you want to shop, try one of these **boutique-lined streets:** rue Paradis, rue de Verdun, rue Masséna, and avenue Jean-Médecin.

Nightlife & Entertainment in Nice

Le Negresco

If you're looking for an elegant place to have a cocktail, try the bar at the Hôtel Negresco. *Info: 37 promenade des Anglais. Tel. 04/93.16.64.12. Open daily 10:30am-1am (until midnight in winter). www.hotel-negresco-nice.com.*

Wayne's

Noisy bar with occasional live performances. It's popular with English-speaking tourists and students. *Info: 15 rue de la Prefecture. Tel. 04/93.13.46.99. Open daily 10am-midnight. www.waynes.fr.*

Casino Palais de Mediterranée

You can gamble the night away at this elegant casino located on the waterfront. Slot machines from 10am. Gaming tables from 8pm. *Info: 15 promenade des Anglais. Tel. 04/92.14.68.00. Open daily. www.casinomediterranee.com.*

Le Ruhl Casino

Recently renovated, you can also gamble the night away at this flashy casino located on the waterfront. There are more than 300 slot machines. *Info: 1 promenade des Anglais. Tel. 04/97.03.12.22. Open daily. www.casinosbarriere.com.*

Events in Nice

• **Carnaval**, Nice's Mardi Gras,
takes place the weeks leading up to Ash Wednesday
• **Nice Jazz Festival**, held for a week in mid-July.
Info: www.nicejazzfestival.fr.

Opéra de Nice
This opulent opera house was designed by Charles Garnier, who also designed the famous opera house in Paris and the casino in Monte Carlo. The four statues on top represent singing, music, dance, and theatre, and the opera house is home to Nice's chorus, orchestra, opera, and ballet. *Info: 4 rue St-François-de-Paule. Tel. 04/92.17.40.00. Tickets available at www.opera-nice.org.*

High Club
You'll pay at least €10 to enter this dance club with three floors. *Info: 45 promenade des Anglais. Tel. 06/16.95.75.87. Open Fri-Sun 11:45pm-6am. www.highclub.fr.*

LGBTQ

Nice is an extremely popular destination for the LGBTQ community. There are a number of popular gay establishments in Nice. Here are just a few:

Le GLAM, Nice's favorite gay nightclub features techno and dance music. There are regular themed parties, including drag shows. *Info: 6 rue Eugène Emmanuel. Tel. 06/60.55.26.61. Thu-Sun 11pm-4am. www.leglamnice.com.*

Red Kafe, 9 rue Halévy, Tel. 04/89.97.47.93 (bar).
Le 7, 7 rue Foncet, Tel. 04/93.62.25.02 (bar).
Le Couloir, 1 rue Alberti (near avenue Felix Faure), Tel. 04/93.85.43.90 (bar).
Les Bains Douches, 16 rue Gubernalis, Tel. 04/93.27.28.72 (sauna).
La Cave Wilson, 7 rue Gubernalis, Tel. 04/93.80.28.26 (bar/cabaret). lacavewilson.fr.
Le Malabar, 10 rue Bonaparte, Tel. 09/51.18.53.52 (bar and café).
Le Morgan, 3 rue Claudia, Tel. 04/93.86.86.08 (cruising bar). www.morganclub.fr.
Le Code, 4 rue Papon, Tel. 09/81.76.86.00 (cruising bar). www.lecodesexclub.com.

The Pride Parade of Nice, the Pink Parade, is held every July. *www.facebook.com/AglaeLGBT/.*

4. EASTERN FRENCH RIVIERA

HIGHLIGHTS

- Slow down in St-Jean-Cap-Ferrat

- An ideal town on the sea: Villefranche-sur-Mer

- Magnificent Eze, peaceful La Turbie, and sedate Menton

- Glitzy Monaco

The French lifestyle with an Italian feel greets you in this part of the French Riviera. The eastern half of the **Côte d'Azur** offers great beaches, beautiful hilltop villages, and renowned gardens.

We'll visit villages east of Nice up to the border and reaching down to the sea. Some of the highlights here include the lovely hilltop village **Eze**, upscale **St-Jean-Cap-Ferrat**, and the quaint harbor town of **Villefranche-sur-Mer**. Visit the unique principality of **Monaco**, or shoot over the border and visit **Ventimiglia** in Italy to eat lunch or shop!

The **Eastern French Riviera** is in the south of France and stretches from the Italian border to Nice along the Mediterranean Sea. The area is about 600 miles (966km) south of Paris. Bus #100 is the best deal if you're using public transportation. It runs from Nice's port (Le Port stop) all the way to Menton on the Italian border. Stops include Villefranche-sur-Mer, Beaulieu-sur-Mer, St-Jean-Cap-Ferrat, Eze- Bord-de-Mer, and Monaco. It doesn't matter how far you travel, the cost is €1.50 each way.

There's a **coastal rail line** that runs from Ventimiglia on the Italian border (Vintimille in French) to Marseille. There are trains that run nearly every hour on this line. Stops on this scenic train ride include: Menton, Cap-Martin, Monaco, Èze-sur-Mer (not to be confused with hilltop Èze), Beaulieu, St-Jean-Cap-Ferrat, Villefranche-sur-Mer, Nice, Antibes and Cannes. Local trains serve many Provence and Riviera towns. You must validate (*composter*) your ticket at a machine (watch locals do it) before you get on a SNCF train.

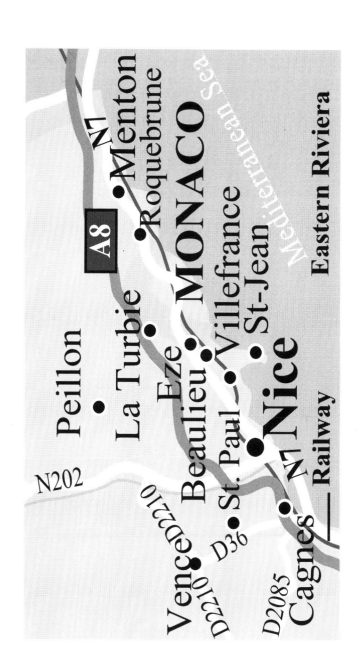

Villefranche-sur-Mer

Villefranche-sur-Mer is a wonderful harbor town, 6 miles (10 km) east of Nice. Bus #100 departs from the port in Nice (Le Port stop) about every 15 minutes. Get off at the Octroi stop to head down to Villefranche-sur-Mer. The cost of the bus ride (which takes less than a half hour) is only €1.50 each way. The train station (with service from most French Riviera towns) is a pleasant 15-minute walk along the water to the Old Town.

The city looks Italian with its yellow and ochre homes reaching down the hill to the sea. The beach here is pebbly, and the deep harbor (located between Nice and Cap Ferrat) can accommodate huge vessels. It's a popular destination for cruise ships.

The interesting **rue Obscure**, a street that runs parallel to the waterfront, is covered by vaulted arcades (it's just off rue de l'Eglise). This "Dark Street" served as a bomb shelter during World War II.

The town has a huge restored citadel (**Citadelle St- Elme**) dating from the 16th-century, housing municipal offices and free museums dedicated to local history and art.

There are **markets** in the Old Town at place Amélie Pollonais. Sunday features antiques (search out the old travel posters). On Saturday there is an organic food market. From Monday to Friday you'll find local crafts, arts, and an interesting flea market.

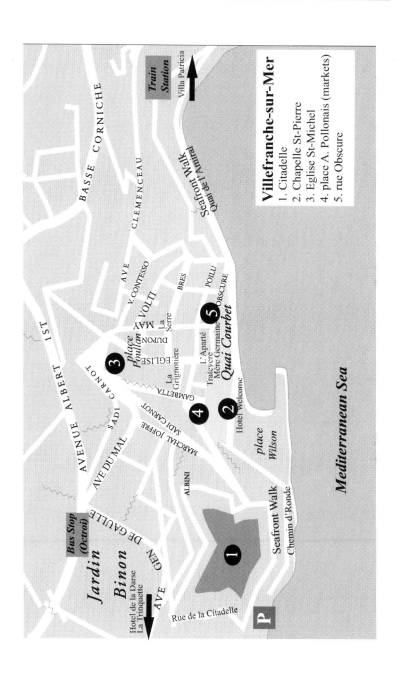

Villefranche-sur-Mer

1. Citadelle
2. Chapelle St-Pierre
3. Eglise St-Michel
4. place A. Pollonais (markets)
5. rue Obscure

Jean Cocteau decorated the walls of **Chapelle St-Pierre**, a Romanesque church, in the 1950s with surrealist works that include images of St. Peter. *Info: quai de la Douane/place Pollonais/rue des Marinières. Tel. 04/93.76.90.70. Closed Mon, Tue, and mid-Nov to mid-Dec. Admission: €3. There are explanations of the art in English.*

Just a few blocks up from the harbor in Old Town is **Eglise St-Michel**. This Baroque church features an 18th-century pipe organ and a stirring statue of Jesus carved from a fig tree. *Info: Place Poullan. Open daily. Admission: Free.*

Hiking/Walking
If you like to walk or hike, Villefranche offers many opportunities.

A walkway along the sea connects the Old Town with the Port de la Darse. As you walk down from the bus stop or road, you'll walk along the Citadelle and at the base turn left to take the walkway to the Old Town.

You can also walk along the sea past the train station for great views of the town. If you're really adventurous, take the 50-minute walk to St-Jean-Cap-Ferrat. You'll need to pass the train station on the small beach lane and then climb the stairs at the end of the beach and walk parallel to the tracks on avenue Bordes. Pass the fabulous villas and take a first right. Watch for the signs to the Villa Rothschild.

Villefranche-sur-Mer Sleeping & Eating
Hôtel Welcome €€€
This former villa has been renovated into a comfortable hotel. All 36 rooms have balconies with views of the port. There is a lively wine bar, and it has an excellent location for exploring the town. *Info: 3 quai Amiral-Courbet. Tel. 04/93.76.27.62. V, MC, AE. Restaurant, bar, AC, TV, minibar, hairdryer, safe, WiFi. www.welcomehotel.com.*

Hôtel de la Darse €

This 21-room hotel is the budget choice in Villefranche. It's located just a little outside of the center of town, so you'll do some walking to get to and from the Old Town. You'll be rewarded for all that walking with excellent sea views. Rooms with garden views are cheapest. *Info: 32 ave. Général de Gaulle. Tel. 04/93.01.72.54. Bar, AC, TV, hairdryer, WiFi. www.hoteldeladarse.com.*

Villa Patricia €-€€

This 10-room seaside hotel is a good choice if you're planning to explore nearby towns by car. Rooms are small (this is France, after all) and clean. There's a lounge where guests can relax. An added bonus is the free parking. It's just a 10-minute walk from Villefranche's Old Town. The owners are extremely helpful. The hotel is located below the Basse Corniche road. *Info: 310 ave. de l'Ange Gardien. Tel. 04/93.01.06.70. TV, WiFi. No AC. www.hotel-patricia-riviera.fr.*

La Mère Germaine €€€

Restaurant on the waterfront specializing in grilled fish dishes. This is the choice for formal dining on the harbor. Try the lobster salad. *Info: quai Courbet. Tel. 04/93.01.71.39. Closed mid-Nov to Dec. www.meregermaine.com.*

La Grignotière €€-€€€

This friendly restaurant is located near the marketplace and serves local specialties. Delicious pasta dishes, especially spaghetti with shrimp (*gambas*). *Info: 3 rue du Poilu. Tel. 04/93.76.79.83. Open daily. www.la-grignotiere-restaurant-villefranche-sur-mer.com.*

Trastevere €€€

This is our favorite restaurant on the harbor. Whether you're having a simple pizza or a delicious pasta dish, you will not be disappointed. Watch locals and tourists departing from boats on the harbor while you sip a glass of Provençal wine. *Info: 7 quai de l'Amiral Courbet. Tel. 04/93.01.94.26. Open daily.*

Le Serre €-€€

You'll find this family-run restaurant in the Old Town near the Eglise St-Michael. You can choose from an assortment of pizzas or one of the specialties like *daube à la niçoise* (beef stew with red wine, tomatoes, and onions). The three-course menu is a good value at around €20. *Info: 16 rue de May. Tel. 04/93.76.79.91. Closed Mon.*

L'Aparté €€-€€€

Located on the interesting medieval rue Obscure, this modern French restaurant serves innovative cuisine. Try the delicious herb-crusted lamb. The wine list features wine from throughout France. *Info: 1 rue Obscure. Tel. 09/83.31.43.62. Closed Sun and Mon. No lunch. www.laparte-villefranche-sur-mer.com.*

La Trinquette €€

At the Port de la Darse (on the other side of the Citadelle from Old Town), this café/restaurant serves locals and tourists in an unpretentious setting along the port. An added bonus is frequent live music. *Info: 30 ave. Général de Gaulle. www.restaurant-trinquette-villefranche.com. Tel. 04/93.16.92.48. Closed Wed. Closed Jan.*

Driving Around

The coastline east of Nice is a huge cliff with three parallel highways (note: if you want to travel at high speeds from the Italian border all the way past Cannes, making day trips easy, take Route A8):

Grande Corniche – the highest and fastest, with the fewest places to enjoy the view.

Moyenne Corniche – the middle road offering shore views and passing through several towns, including the beautiful and popular Èze.

Basse Corniche – the lowest where you might crawl (especially in July and August) through one picturesque resort after another.

St-Jean-Cap-Ferrat

We're going to slow down in **St-Jean-Cap-Ferrat**, 1 mile (2 km) south of Beaulieu/6 miles (10 km) east of Nice.

The residents of this port village on the peninsula Cap-Ferrat live here for its warm climate and beautiful sea views. Its promenades are lined with cafés and restaurants, and its port is filled with pleasure craft. It's home to luxurious hotels including the **Grand Hôtel du Cap-Ferrat**, located at the tip of the peninsula. Most of the villas are hidden by gates and lush vegetation. Unlike nearby towns, the pace here is not at all hectic. The beaches are pebbly, not sandy, and there's a coastal walkway if you want to walk around the cape.

While here, visit the **Villa Ephrussi de Rothschild/Musée Ile-de-France**, a sumptuous palace by the sea. This Italian-style villa was left to the French government by Baroness Rothschild, and includes over 5,000 works of art.

Fabulous gardens with ornamental lakes and waterfalls surround the villa. *Info: avenue Denis-Séméria. Tel. 04/93.01.33.09. Open daily 10am-6pm (Jul and Aug until 7pm). Nov to Jan Mon-Fri 2pm-6pm, Sat and Sun 10am-6pm. Admission: €16 (with English audioguide). www.villa-ephrussi.com.*

St-Jean-Cap-Ferrat Sleeping & Eating

Grand Hôtel du Cap-Ferrat (Four Seasons) €€€
Luxurious white palace set in the middle of a 17-acre wooded estate and subtropical gardens. Its exclusive location is at the tip of the Cap-Ferrat peninsula. Every amenity you can imagine is here. A nice bonus: great views of the sea from its clifftop pool. *Info: St-Jean-Cap-Ferrat. Tel. 04/93.76.50.50. V, MC, DC, AE. Restaurant, bar, outdoor pool, TV, telephone, minibar, hairdryer, safe, WiFi. www.fourseasons.com.*

Hotel Brise Marine €€
Lovely yellow hotel located in a former villa with a fantastic porch and patio overlooking the water. Great place to unwind. Rooms are comfortable and casual. Highly recommended. *Info: 58 avenue Jean Mermoz. Tel. 04/93.76.04.36. V, MC, DC, AE. Bar, TV, telephone, WiFi. www.hotel-brisemarine.com.*

Capitaine Cook €€-€€€
Hearty Provençal dining indoors and outdoors on the patio. This is a family-run restaurant specializing in fish dishes. Try the delicious salmon ravioli. *Info: 11 av. Jean-Mermoz. Tel. 04/93.76.02.66. Closed Wed.*

Le Pacha du Sloop - Chez Fifi €€-€€€
You can't miss the blue-and-white décor of this portside restaurant. Fish dishes are featured at the indoor and outdoor tables. Excellent *soupe de poisson* (fish soup). *Info: On the port. Tel. 04/93.01.48.63. Closed Tue and Wed. www.le-pacha-du-sloop-restaurant-st-jean-cap-ferrat.com.*

Beaulieu-sur-Mer
Beaulieu-sur-Mer is just two miles (four km) east of Villefranche-sur-Mer.

This village is referred to as "La Petite Afrique" (Little Africa) owing to its warm climate and lush vegetation. The Alpes-Maritimes mountains descending to the coast shelter this resort town. The stroll along the seafront promenade lets you glimpse lovely villas, most of which are hidden by vegetation and fences. The Art Deco **Casino de Beaulieu** was built in 1903 (no beach attire). The town has two churches, the 12th-century chapel **Santa Maria de Olivo**, and the 19th-century **Eglise du Sacré-Coeur**.

In a town with incredible villas, the **Villa Kérylos** stands out. Step inside for a look. It's an imitation of a Greek villa from Classical times, and contains some Greek antiquities brought here in 1900 when the villa was built by an archeologist. Definitely unusual! *Info: rue Gustave-Eiffel (at the tip of the bay). Tel. 04/93.01.01.44. Open daily Sep-Apr 10am-5pm (May-Aug until 5:30pm). Admission: €11.50 (with English audio guide). www.villakerylos.fr.*

Beaulieu-sur-Mer Sleeping & Eating
La Pignatelle €€
Dine indoors or outdoors with locals at this restaurant located off of the main street. Nothing fancy here. Featured dishes include *gibelotte de laupin* (rabbit stew) and *tartare de saumon* (salmon tartar). A good deal in expensive Beaulieu. *Info: 10 rue de Quincenet. Tel. 04/93.01.03.37. Closed Sun lunch. www.lapignatelle.fr.*

La Reserve de Beaulieu €€€
The luxury hotel in lovely Beaulieu. This hotel, with a pink-and-white exterior and marble lobby welcomes guests who want to be pampered. It's known for its spa. Every amenity imaginable is available. The highlight is the fabulous 2000-square-foot pool and the sun deck overlooking the sea. Most rooms have balconies where you can take in the Mediterranean Sea. *Info: 5 Boulevard du Marechal Leclerc. Tel. 04/93.01.00.01. V, MC, AE. Spa, restaurants, bar, AC, TV, safe, minibar, WiFi. www.reservebeaulieu.com.*

La Reserve also is known for its restaurants and bars. Our favorite is the **pool bar** with its idyllic setting overlooking the sea and coast. You'll pay for your lunch and drinks here, but it's truly a fantastic setting. Pool bar is open daily 9am-6pm. The formal **Gordon Bennett Bar**, with plush chairs and wood paneling, also serves food and drink. Elegant (and expensive) dining is served at the other restaurants: **Restaurant des Rois** (award-winning restaurant), **La Table de la Réserve** (bistro), and **Le Vent Debout** (summer restaurant).

Le Havre Bleu €
There are plenty of luxury hotels in Beaulieu, but this is not one of them. This small hotel, with blue shutters, offers simple rooms in a central location. Ask for a room with a terrace or patio. Excellent value. *Info: 29 blvd. Maréchal Joffre. Tel. 04/93.01.01.40. V, MC, AE. Bar, AC, TV, WiFi. www.lehavrebleu.com.*

Eze

Today you'll visit the most magnificent hilltop village, **Eze**. It's 4 miles (7 km) west of Monte Carlo/7 miles (11 km) east of Nice (via the Moyenne Corniche).

To say that Eze has a magnificent hilltop location is an understatement. This tiny fortified village towers over the surrounding countryside with unbelievable views of the sea. It's the highest of the area's perched villages. You'll enter through the town gate (designed to keep the Turks out). Most of this rocky village dates back to the 14th century. On your way to the top is the tiny **Chapelle de la Ste-Croix**, the former seat of a lay brotherhood that wore white habits and performed good deeds The church of **Notre-Dame de l'Assomption** (built in 1764) has a Baroque interior. A web of narrow streets passes stone houses converted to boutiques, galleries, and souvenir shops. It's touristy and, in high season, the narrow streets can get quite cramped, but the view from the hilltop castle ruins are worth it.

For the adventurous, there's a walk on an old mule trail from Eze to **Eze-Bord-de-Mer** on the coast. Look for signs for **Sentier Fédéric Nietzsche**. You begin at the entry to town (just to the left of the entrance to the luxury hotel Château de la Chèvre d'Or). The walk takes at least an hour each way and although beautiful, is only for the fit. If you're not up to the entire walk, just head down a bit for a great view of the coast.

Make sure to visit the **Jardin Exotique** at the hilltop castle ruins. This densely planted flower and cactus garden (with English descriptions), along with whimsical statuary, affords spectacular views. Don't miss it! *Info: Tel. 04/93.41.10.30. Open daily 9am-sunset. Admission: €6. www.jardinexotique-eze.fr.*

Eze Sleeping & Eating

Château Eza €€€
This former residence of Prince William of Sweden is now an elegant hotel built into the medieval walls. Donkeys carry your luggage up the narrow and steep cobblestone street. There are only 10 rooms. Extraordinary views. *Info: Rue de la Pise. Tel. 04/93.41.12.24. V, MC, DC, AE. Restaurant, bar, AC, TV, telephone, minibar, in-room safe, hairdryer, WiFi. www.chateaueza.com.*

Hostellerie du Château de la Chèvre d'Or €€€€
This incredible luxury-hotel complex of stone houses has 32 rooms. Its secluded setting with narrow alleys has great views of the sea. Truly a unique (and expensive) vacation experience. Its restaurants and outdoor cliffside bar are just the place to splurge. Fabulous infinity pool. *Info: rue du Barri. Tel. 04/92.10.66.66. V, MC, DC, AE. Restaurant, bar, gym, AC, TV, telephone, minibar, in-room safe, hairdryer.www.chevredor.com.*

La Vieille Maison €€
This family restaurant is located in the seafront town of Eze-sur-Mer. It's a rarity in the area around Eze as it's reasonably priced. Regional dishes are served with affordable local wines. Dine on the rooftop terrace with great views. Known for their *moules* (mussels) and delicious *frites* (French fries served with mayonnaise). *Info: 18 ave. de la Liberté in Èze-Bord-de-Mer. Tel. 04/93.01.58.30. Closed Sun.*

Restaurant de la Chèvre d'Or €€€
This award-winning restaurant in the Hostellerie du Château de la Chèvre d'Or is one of the best in the French Riviera. The menu features innovative Mediterranean dishes prepared by its star chef. The wine cellar boasts over 20,000 bottles from throughout France. Marble floors, cherry wood paneling, impeccable service, and magnificent panoramic views all add to the experience. *Info: Hostellerie du Château de la Chèvre d'Or. Reservations required. Tel. 04/92.10.66.61. Closed Dec to mid-Mar. www.chevredor.com.*

Have a drink at sunset at the outdoor **cliffside hotel bar**. But be warned—there's a steep minimum drink order on weekends. *Info: rue du Barri. Tel. 04/92.10.66.66. Closed mid-Nov to Feb.*

Monaco
Monaco, the capital of glitz, is 12 miles (19 km) east of Nice. Bus #100 connects Monaco to Nice and Menton (and points between) for €1.50. The bus departs from Le Port stop in Nice at the Port de Nice (at the top of the Port across from the church Notre-Dame du Port). The bus runs every 15 minutes. By train, you can reach Monaco from Nice (two per hour/25-minute trip), Villefranche (two per hour/15-minute trip), Antibes (two per hour/60-minute trip), and Cannes (two per hour/70-minute trip).

Monaco mixes aristocratic glitz and a little bit of Las Vegas. It's the second-smallest state in Europe; only Vatican City is smaller. This principality is bordered by France and the Mediterranean Sea, takes up less than one square mile, and is nestled

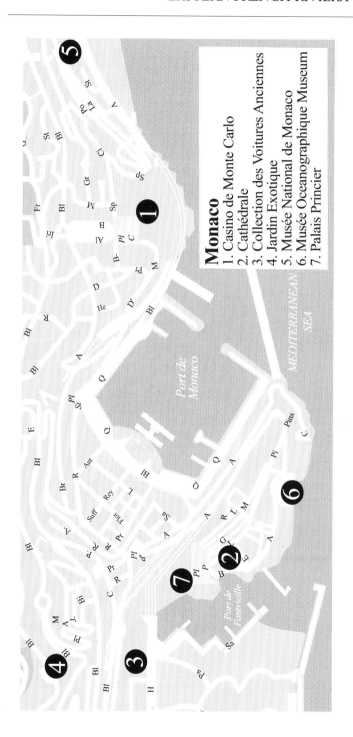

Monaco
1. Casino de Monte Carlo
2. Cathédrale
3. Collection des Voitures Anciennes
4. Jardin Exotique
5. Musée National de Monaco
6. Musée Oceanographique Museum
7. Palais Princier

against mountains that seem to push it into the sea. High-rises attest to the fact that there's nowhere to go but up in this tiny country. Residents (Monégasques), of which there are less than 10,000, pay no taxes.

There are four parts of the principality: **Monte Carlo**, home to the famous casino and ultra-luxury hotels; **Fontvieille**, an industrial suburb; **Monaco-Ville**, the location of government buildings and the royal palace; and **La Condamine**, at the port where most Monégasques live.

Monaco's location is fantastic, its weather incredible (on average, 310 sunny days a year) and crime is virtually unheard of (there's one policeman for every 100 residents).

Bus service is available within Monaco for €2, day pass €6.25), with stops at every tourist sight. To figure out which one to take, simply look at the name on the front of the bus.

Grace Kelly

American film star **Grace Kelly** met Prince Rainier of Monaco while attending the Cannes International Film Festival to promote the Alfred Hitchcock film *To Catch a Thief*, which she starred in with Cary Grant. The film featured her racing along the Corniches. Soon after, in 1956, she married Prince Rainier, moved to Monaco, and had three children with him. Princess Grace was wildly popular among the Monégasques. Ironically, in 1982 she was killed while driving on the same Corniches featured in her film. The flower-decked tomb of Princess Grace is located at **Cathédrale de l'Immaculée-Conception**, a Romanesque-style church, which was also the site of her fairy-tale wedding to Prince Rainier in 1956. Prince Rainier was buried at her side in 2005. *Info: avenue St-Martin. Open daily. Admission: Free.*

Head to the **Place du Palais**. This square offers views of the palace and contains a **statue of Francesco Grimaldi**. Francesco (they refer to him as François here) was an Italian who was kicked out of Genoa.

He and his cohorts dressed up as monks in 1297 and seized the castle. This was the beginning of the Grimaldi dynasty, which continues to this day.

You can't miss **Le Rocher** (The Rock), crowned by the Prince's Palace. A medieval castle once stood where the **Palais Princier** is located. In the summer you can take a guided tour through the royal family's extravagant home. Included in the tour is a glimpse of the immense art collection, the throne room, the **royal apartments** (Les Grands Appartements), and the beautiful state portrait of Princess Grace. You can watch the colorful changing of the guard at around 11:45am to noon. *Info: place du Palais. Tel. 377/93.25.18.31. Royal apartments: Open Apr to mid-Oct 10am-5:30pm (Jul and Aug until 6:30pm). Closed mid-Oct to Mar. Admission: €10. www.palais.mc.*

The **Musée Océanographique** (Oceanography Museum), built in 1910, hangs from a cliff in Monaco-Ville. It's sometimes referred to as the Cousteau Aquarium, as Jacques Cousteau, the famous sea-explorer, directed the aquarium until 1988. In addition to its huge (over 90 tanks) and interesting aquarium, the museum contains skeletons of sea creatures (including a giant whale), submarines, and exhibits on the history of sea exploration. *Info: avenue St-Martin. Tel. 377/93.15.36.00. Open daily Jul and Aug 9:30am-8pm, Apr-Jun and Sep 10am-7pm, Oct-Mar 10am-6pm. Admission: €18, €12 ages 6-17, €8 ages 4-12. www.oceano.mc.*

The **Jardin Exotique** is an exotic garden with thousands of cacti and succulents. Incredible views of the coast are included in the admission price. *Info: boulevard du Jardin Exotique. Tel. 377/93.15.29.80. Closed through 2022. Greenhouses open with free access Tue-Sat 8:30am-3:30pm. www.jardin-exotique.mc.*

Nouveau Musée National de Monaco

Rotating exhibits (with an emphasis on artists who visited Monaco and on the history of Monaco) are held at two locations. Villa Sauber is located in a luxurious villa (designed by the same man who designed the Casino de Monte Carlo). *Info: Villa Sauber is east of the casino at 17 avenue Princess Grace. Tel. 377/93.30.91.26. Villa Paloma is next to the Jardin Exotique at 56 blvd. du Jardin. Tel. 377/98.98.48.60. Both open daily 10am-6pm. Admission: €6. Free Sun and Tue 12:30pm-2pm. www.nmnm.mc.*

Collection des Voitures Anciennes
(Collection of Antique Cars)

The royal collection of over 100 automobiles. Now do they need both a Rolls Royce and a Lamborghini? *Info: Les Terrasses de Fontvieille. Tel. 377/92.05.28.56. Open daily 10am-6pm. Admission: €8. www.palais.mc.*

There's **great shopping** in Monaco. Main shopping streets include **boulevard des Moulins** (the main street of Monte Carlo), **rue Princess-Caroline** (everything from clothing to baked goods) and **rue Grimaldi** (the main shopping street of the La Condamine area). At **place d'Armes** there is an indoor and outdoor market (every morning).

If you want to shop and feel good about parting with your cash, check out **Boutique du Rocher** at 1 avenue de la Madone. This boutique was established by Princess Grace to provide an outlet for Monégasque products (everything from linens to dolls). Some products are created at workshops here. The profits all go to the Princess Grace Charitable Foundation. *Tel. 377/93.30.91.17. Closed Sun.*

Le Jardin Animalier (Zoological Gardens)

This zoo is on the southern side of Le Rocher. Hundreds of animals, including lemurs, turtles, and hippopatumus have found shelter here. All the animals are donated, abandoned, or were seized by customs. *Info: Esplanade Ranier III. Tel. 377/93.50.40.30. Open daily 10am-noon and 2pm-6pm (Jun-Sep 9am-noon and 2pm-7pm). Admission: €6.*

Casino de Monte Carlo

Charles Garnier, who designed the opulent Paris Opera House, designed the casino in 1878. Appropriately, there's an opera house inside the casino.

The marble atrium with 28 Ionic columns welcomes you (for free). The **Salle Garnier** (named after the architect) is a red-and-gold, opulent concert hall with an 18-ton chandelier. The **Salon Blanc** has painted muses.

Perhaps the most interesting room is the **Salon Rose** (the smoking room). Its ceiling is decorated with cigar-smoking female nudes. Roulette is played in both the **Salle Européen**, with its eight gigantic chandeliers, and in the ornate Renaissance Hall. The private rooms (**Salles Privées**) are where high rollers gamble surrounded by carved mahogany. The **Salle Américaine** (free admission) opens early (at noon) and has Las Vegas-style slot machines. It's without a doubt the world's most glamorous casino.

Outside are immaculately maintained gardens, and, in front of the casino, the Art Deco **Café de Paris** where you can sip a pricey mimosa or enjoy a crêpe Suzette. *Info: place du Casino. Tel. 377/98.06.41.51. Open daily for gaming after 2pm. Admission: €10. www.montecarlosbm.com.*

Hôtel de Paris

Okay, this is a hotel, not a sight. Or is it? Even if you can't afford to stay here or even eat or drink here, you should at least pop in and be dazzled by the magnificent domed entrance. The palatial lobby is a masterpiece of stained glass, statues, crystal chandeliers, and marble pillars. It's said that if you rub the raised knee of the bronze statue of Louis XIV's horse in the lobby, you'll have good luck.

Monaco Happenings

The Spring Arts Festival (**Printemps des Arts**) featuring symphonic, opera and ballet performances is held each spring.

The **Monte Carlo Tennis Tournament** is held in April.

The famous auto race **Grand Prix de Monaco** takes place in mid-May.

Each June, Monte Carlo hosts the International Festival of Television (**Le Festival International de la Télévision**), the television version of the Cannes Film Festival.

Monaco Sleeping & Eating

Hôtel de Paris €€€
You'll be dazzled by the magnificent domed entrance. The palatial lobby is a masterpiece of stained glass, statues, crystal chandeliers, and marble pillars, and the rooms and service match the elegance of the common areas. *Info: place du Casino (opposite the casino). Tel. 377/98.06.20.00. V, MC, AE. Restaurant, bar, AC, TV, telephone, minibar, in-room safe, hairdryer, WiFi. www.montecarlosbm.com.*

Hôtel Ambassador €€
Not everyone can afford to stay at the glamorous Hôtel de Paris or the other exclusive hotels here, and it's not easy to find affordable hotels in this glitzy place. But, this 35-unit hotel has comfortable, if not small, rooms in the Condamine district. *Info: 25 Ave. Prince Pierre. Tel. 377/97.97.96.96. V, MC, AE. Bar, AC, TV, telephone, WiFi. www.ambassadormonaco.com.*

Le Louis XV- Alain Ducasse €€€
This restaurant in the luxurious Hôtel de Paris is run by famous chef Alain Ducasse. Innovative French and Italian cuisine and attentive service. *Info: place du Casino in the Hôtel de Paris. Tel. 377/98.06.88.64. Closed Wed. Reservations required. www.montecarlosbm.com.*

Loga €€-€€€
This bistro serving Mediterranean fare will not disappoint. Come here for *barbajuans*, the national dish of Monaco. It's ravioli stuffed with chard and ricotta. Delicious! You can dine inside or on the terrace along the shopping street boulevard des Moulins. *Info: 25 blvd des Moulins. Tel. 377/93.30.87.72. Closed Wed (dinner), Sun, and part of Aug. www.logarestaurant.com.*

Stars 'n Bars €€
Yearning for a little taste of home? Try this American-style sports bar. *Info: 6 quai Antoine-1er. Tel. 377/97.97.95.95. Open daily. www.starsnbars.com.*

The Hill Towns Above Monaco
If you've visited Monaco, you may just want to take it easy in peaceful hill towns. We'll start in **La Turbie**. It's 7 miles (11 km) northeast of Nice (via the Grande Corniche).

There's something very peaceful about La Turbie, located in the hills above the coast. It's not as touristy as nearby Eze, and it certainly is quieter than the coastal towns. The massive Roman monument **La Trophée des Alpes** (The Trophy of the Alps) was built in 6 B.C. to celebrate Augustus Caesar's conquest of the Alps. A small museum near the monument, Musée du Trophée des Alpes, describes the history of the monument and its restoration. *Info: www.trophee-auguste.fr. Tel. 04/93.41.20.84. Open 10am-1:30pm and 2:30pm-5pm (summer 9:30am-1pm and 2:30pm-6:30pm).Closed Mon. Admission: €6.* See photo on next page.

After La Turbie, follow the signs to **Peillon**. It's 11 miles (18 km) northeast of Nice.

Peillon is a perched village, but unlike so many of the others, it's void of touristy boutiques. Why? It's hard to get to. You may feel like you've stepped back into medieval times. There's only one gateway into this village of ancient homes with red-tiled roofs. You can visit the Baroque church **Eglise St- Saveur** and **Chapelle des Pénitents Blancs**, a chapel with frescoes of the passion of Christ, dating back to the late 15th century.

Though not as unspoiled as Peillon, nearby **Roquebrune** will allow you to wander in relative peace. It's three miles (five km) west of Menton/three miles (five km) east of Monaco, located along the Grande Corniche. The entire village has been renovated, and its steep alleys and arcaded lanes are filled with galleries, boutiques, and souvenir shops. The castle on the hilltop is said to be the oldest feudal castle in France, built over 1,000 years ago. You can also visit the 12th-century **Eglise Ste-Marguerite**. The long and narrow street **rue Moncollet** is lined with houses dating back to the Middle Ages. Just outside the village stands the **Olivier Millénaire**, a thousand-year-old olive tree, said to be the oldest tree in the world.

The **Château de Roquebrune** is the oldest feudal castle in France. It's dominated by two square towers (with fantastic views of the coast). Inside is a museum tracing the castle's history. *Info: rue du Château. Tel. 04/93.35.07.22. Closed Thu and Fri Oct-Jun. Admission: €5. www.roquebrune-cap-martin.fr.*

Cap-Martin, 1 1/2 miles west of Roquebrune, is a wealthy, mostly residential seaside resort.

Roquebrune Sleeping & Eating
Les Deux Frères €€
Some of the ten guest rooms at this inn have views of the Mediterranean Sea below. You'll be staying in a converted schoolhouse. The Dutch owners provide a friendly welcome and although the rooms are small, the price is right. *Info: 1 place des Deux Frères. Tel. 04/93.28.91.00. V, MC, AE. Restaurant, AC, TV. les-deux-freres.leprovence-hotel.com.*

The restaurant here (€€€) will not disappoint. Excellent French, Italian, and Mediterranean dishes. Try the *carré d'agneau* (rack of lamb). Extensive wine list featuring local producers.

Au Grand Inquisiteur €€-€€€
Up a steep stairway on your way to the feudal castle, you'll find this small restaurant in a cellar. Good Provençal cooking with a huge wine list. Try the *noisette de cerf grillé* (grilled venison). Note that sometimes it's closed for lunch. *Info: 18 rue du Château. Tel. 04/93.35.05.37. Closed Wed. www.augrandinquisiteur.com.*

Menton

Depending on which way you look at it, **Menton** is either at the end or the beginning of the French Riviera. It's five miles (nine km) east of Monaco. Menton doesn't feel very French. This isn't solely because of its location on the Italian border, but also a result of the large number of expatriates who have come to Menton to retire. Its climate is the warmest of all the towns in this book, warm enough to grow citrus fruits, and there's a huge Lemon Festival (**Fête du Citron**) held every February. Legend has it that when Adam and Eve were kicked out of the Garden of Eden, Eve snuck out a lemon and planted it in Menton (because the town reminded her of her former home). There are many lovely gardens in the city. Its long **Promenade du Soleil** (on the **Golfe de la Paix**) runs along a narrow pebble beach and the main costal road. Menton's Old Town, with narrow streets and main street **rue St-Michel**, is on the east side of town. It's sedate, but has much to offer the traveler. *Info: www.menton.fr.*

There are several museums worth visiting here.

The **Musée des Beaux-Arts** (a fine-arts museum) contains European paintings from the Renaissance to present day. But the real attraction here are the grounds of the **Palais Carnoles**. The gardens of this 18th-century palace (once the summer home of the Princess of Monaco) are filled with orange, grapefruit, and lemon trees. *Info: 3 avenue de la Madone (in the Palais Carnoles). Tel. 04/93.35.49.71. Closed Tue. Admission: Free. Currently closed for renovations.*

The **Musée de Préhistoire Régionale** is dedicated to human evolution. Its highlight is the head of a prehistoric man found in 1884 in nearby caves. *Info: rue Lorédan-Larchey. Tel. 04/89.81.52.12. Open 10am-noon and 2pm-6pm. Closed Tue. Admission: €3. www.menton.fr.*

The **Musée Jean-Cocteau** (sometimes called the Bastion museum) is devoted to the works of writer and artist Jean-Cocteau. It's located in the Bastion du Port, a 17th-century fortress on the port. Cocteau coordinated the restoration of the fortress. *Info: Vieux Port. Info: Tel. 04/93.18.82.61. Open 10am-12:30pm and 2pm-6pm. Closed Tue. Admission: €3.* Another museum dedicated to Cocteau (www.museecocteaumenton.fr) is on the waterfront. *Currently closed for renovations.* Cocteau also adorned the walls and ceiling of the town hall on place Ardoïno.

If you have time, pop into the **Basilique St-Michel.** The bell tower of this Baroque church can be seen throughout Menton. The richly decorated basilica has a huge 17th-century organ. Nearby is the splendid **Chapelle de l'Immaculée-Conception,** dating back to the 1600s. *Info: Parvis St-Michel. Open daily. Admission: Free.*

In the Old Town between rue St-Michel and the sea is the beautiful **Marché Couvert** (Covered Market). Cheese, fruits, French breads and Italian specialties can all be found here.

Menton Sleeping & Eating
Hôtel Riva €€
Hotel Riva enjoys a great location close to the city center and just opposite the sea. Guests can enjoy the top floor sun deck. There's also a spa at the hotel. You'll be close to the sights of Menton and have easy access to the promenade along the sea (which you can follow all the way to Monaco). *Info: 600 Promenade du Soleil. Tel. 04/92.10.92.10. , MC, AE. Bar, AC, TV, telephone, WiFi. Parking is available for a fee. www.rivahotel.com.*

La Trattoria €€
Menton was part of Italy until 1860 and you'll see the Italian influence in everything from architecture to cuisine. This restaurant near the Port of Menton serves Italian, Provençal and French food (especially seafood). Good house wine served by the *pichet* (pitcher). *Info: 15 avenue de Verdun. Tel. 09/83.61.60.91. Open daily. www. latrottoria-menton.fr.*

Ventimiglia, Italy
Much of the French Riviera was part of Italy until 1860, so you'll see the Italian influence in everything from architecture to cuisine.

Just across the border from Menton is the Italian town of **Ventimiglia** (Vintimille in French). Why not head here for lunch, so when you return from your trip, you can tell friends that you had lunch in Italy? It has a lovely **Città Vecchia** (Old Town), an 11th-century **Duomo** (cathedral), and many restaurants to choose from. Be warned that traffic can be chaotic on Fridays when there's a vast **mercato** (market) selling everything from flowers to leather goods.

5. WESTERN FRENCH RIVIERA

HIGHLIGHTS

- A St-Tropez tan and glamorous Cannes

- The ancient town of Antibes

- The incredible clifftop village of Gourdon

- St-Paul-de-Vence, the most visited village in France

The **Côte d'Azur** got its name from a guidebook written in 1887 covering the area from the Italian border to Hyères. The author was referring to the coast's clear blue skies, not, as many think, to the blue waters of the Mediterranean Sea. Most English speakers call this area the French Riviera. Hilltop villages, art museums, coastal resorts, and a St-Tropez tan all await you in the western French Riviera.

If you can, visit after the high-season onslaught of tourists in July and August. It's easier to drive on the corniches and easier to park in the small villages. The temperatures are comfortable, and life, especially in smaller towns, returns to normal. In some areas, especially seaside resorts, many places close during November and December.

Once just a quiet fishing village and favorite of artists, **St-Tropez** burst on the world scene when sexy Brigitte Bardot arrived in her sunglasses and capri pants to star in the 1950s film *And God Created Woman*. Despite its reputation as a tourist mecca for the beautiful, rich, and famous, it still retains much of its charm. Nearby, you'll find picturesque villages and great beaches in places like **Grimaud**, **Antibes**, and **Cannes**.

The **western French Riviera** is in the south of France and stretches from Nice to St-Tropez. The area is about 600 miles (966km) south of Paris. From Nice, there is bus service to Antibes (#250) and Cannes (#210), St-Paul-de-Vence and Vence (#400), and Grasse (#500). *nice-airport.net/bus.php.* Train service from Nice includes Cannes (25-40 minutes). *sncf.com.*

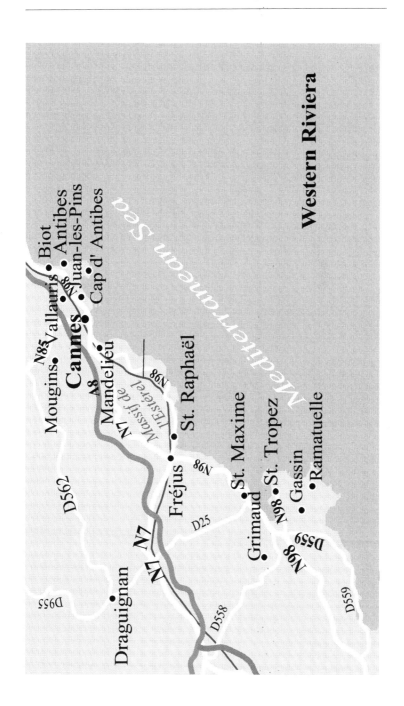

St-Tropez

Let's get a tan in **St-Tropez**. It's 41 miles (66 km) northeast of Toulon/22 miles (35 km) southwest of Fréjus/47 miles (76 km) southwest of Cannes.

Come here to sit in the Old Port (**Vieux Port**) along the quai Jean-Jaurès, where yachts from all over the world dock, and enjoy some of the world's best people-watching. St-Tropez's web of narrow streets in the Old Town (**Quartier de la Ponche**) are lined with pastel-painted buildings with red-tile roofs filled with restaurants and boutiques for every budget (especially those with an unlimited budget). You can't miss **Eglise St-Tropez**'s bell tower painted in yellow and orange. Oh, and for that St-Tropez tan, there are some great beaches here, too!

Head for the **Place des Lices** along boulevard Vasserot. Cafés shaded by plane trees line this market square. On Tuesday and Saturday mornings, it's filled with stalls selling everything from produce to antiques. In the evening, you can witness the evening promenade, where locals walk and greet each other.

There's one museum that's a must-see when you want to take a break from shopping and the beaches: The **Musée de l'Annonciade/Musée St-Tropez**. This 14th-century chapel is now a wonderful art museum. You'll find a superb collection of Impressionist and Post-Impressionist paintings by Signac,

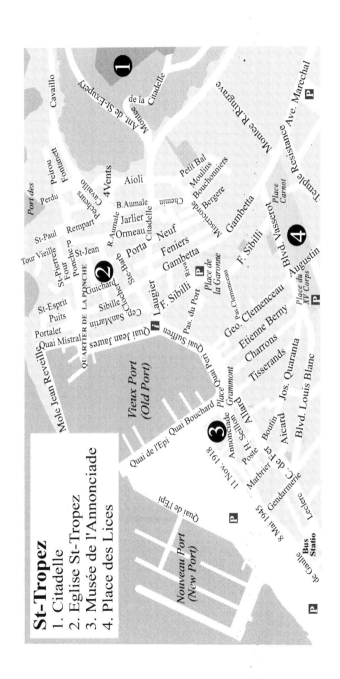

St-Tropez
1. Citadelle
2. Eglise St-Tropez
3. Musée de l'Annonciade
4. Place des Lices

Matisse and Dufy, to name a few. What makes this museum interesting is that many of the paintings are actually of St-Tropez. *Info: place Grammont (near the Old Port). Tel. 04/94.17.84.10. Open 10am-6pm (July-Sep until 7pm). Closed Mon. Admission: €6.*

You may want to visit the **Citadelle**, where 17th-century ramparts surround this fort. Come here to take in the view of the town and coast and enjoy the quiet park. *Info: rue de la Citadelle.*

It's the sun and beaches (*les plages*) that attract many visitors to St-Tropez. **Plage de la Bouillabaisse** (don't you love that name?) and **plage des Graniers** are closest to town, accessible by foot, and popular with families.

The **Route des Plages** (Beach Road) takes you to some of the best beaches that begin 2 1/2 miles (4 km) south of town at the plage des Salins, accessible by bicycle or car. **Plage des Tahiti** is a favorite with nudists, and Coco Beach (toward Ramatuelle) is popular with the LGBTQ community. You'll find bars, restaurants and shops at popular and packed **plage de Pampelonne**. A simple beach seafood restaurant? Ask one of the many celebrities that have stopped at **Le Club 55** on place de Pampelonne. www.club55.fr.

St-Tropez Sleeping & Eating
Le Byblos €€€
Trying to get into one of the 52 rooms or 43 suites at this hotel can be a challenge (almost as hard as getting into its Caves du Roy nightclub). If you manage to get in, you'll share the place with celebrities and guests on expense accounts. Modern, comfortable, and glamorous. There are two restaurants, both highly acclaimed and expensive: Arcadia and Cucina (27 ave. Foch). *Info: Ave. Paul-Signac. Tel. 04/94.56.68.00. V, MC, DC, AE. Restaurants, bar, outdoor pool, AC, cable TV, telephone, gym, minibar, hairdryer, safe, WiFi. www.byblos.com.*

Hôtel Le Yaca €€€

This former private home was built in 1722. It was once the meeting place of Impressionist painters such as Paul Signac. The 28-room hotel is situated on a small street in the Old Town. Many of the rooms have views of the beautiful inner flower garden. Upper-floor rooms have views of the Gulf of St-Tropez. In July and August, there's a shuttle service to the beach (or you can just hang out at the beautiful swimming pool). *Info: 1 blvd. D'Aumale. Tel. 04/94.55.81.00. V, MC, DC, AE. Restaurant, bar, outdoor pool, AC, TV, telephone, minibar, hairdryer, safe, WiFi. Closed mid-Oct to mid-Apr. www.hotel-le-yaca.fr.*

Hôtel Sube €€

Located on the port near the tourist office, this hotel has a lovely lounge and comfortable rooms (you'll pay more for a port view). Great location for shopping. *Info: 15 quai Suffren. Tel. 04/94.97.30.04. V, MC, AE. Bar, AC, TV, telephone. www.hotelsubesainttropez.com.*

Lou Cagnard €-€€

This 19-room hotel is located in a renovated villa. It's family-owned and you'll have a warm welcome. Good central location. There's a lovely garden surrounded by fig trees where you can relax or have breakfast (extra charge). Note that a few of the rooms do not have air conditioning. *Info: 18 ave. Paul-Poussel. Tel. 04/94.97.04.24. V, MC. AC, TV, telephone, safe, free parking. Closed Nov-Feb. www.hotel-lou-cagnard.com.*

Le Girelier €€-€€€

Grilled fish is the specialty at this restaurant on the port. Try the *saumon à la plancha* (grilled salmon). *Info: quai Jean-Jaurès (on the harbor). Tel. 04/94.97.03.87. Closed mid-Nov to mid-Dec. www.legirelier.fr.*

Le Club 55 €€-€€€

A simple beachside seafood restaurant? Ask one of the celebrities that have eaten here. There's also a great shop selling everything you need for the beach. *Info: 55 boulevard Patch. plage de Pampelonne. Tel. 04/94.55.55.55. www.club55.fr.*

Le Magnan €€
Ten minutes from St-Tropez in Cogolin, this restaurant specializes in Provençal country cooking and is located on a hilltop farm. Try the *epaule d'agneau confite 7 heures* (shoulder of lamb cooked seven hours). Definitely worth the drive. *Info: On route N98 in Cogolin (6 miles (9 km) west of St-Tropez). Tel. 04/94.49.57.54. Closed Mon-Wed and mid-Nov to Feb. www.lemagnan.fr.*

St-Tropez Nightlife & Entertainment
Les Caves du Roy
If you can get in, you can drink and dance the night away at this bar/club in the Byblos Hotel. *Info: Ave. du Marechal Foch. www.lescavesduroy.com. Open weekends Apr-Oct. Open nightly Jul and Aug.*

St-Tropez Shopping
Kiwi
Towels, bags, espadrilles, and sexy beach wear. *Info: 34 rue Allard. Tel 04/94.97.42.26. www.kiwi.fr.*

Galeries Tropéziennes
Clothes, home goods, and unusual gifts at one of the oldest shops in the city. Known for their selection of purses. *Info: 82 rue Gambetta. Tel. 04/94.97.02.21. www.galeriestropeziennes.com.*

Around the Gulf of St-Tropez

While St-Tropez is fabulous, don't ignore the area around it. Today we'll visit nearby gulf towns and picturesque villages (especially Grimaud). There's something for families, those looking for beach resorts, or those who want to spend their days on the golf course.

For families, head to **Ste-Maxime**, 7 miles (12 km) east of St-Tropez. This modern resort town directly on the Gulf of St-Tropez (across from St-Tropez) is sheltered by the Maures Mountains. The town is popular with families, and overall is much cheaper than glitzy St-Tropez. There's a large waterfront promenade and a small Old Town. You can view the **Eglise Ste-Maxime**, a 15th-century church, and the **Tour Carrée des Dames** (Dames Tower), a 16th-century tower that houses a museum dedicated to local history. Befitting a resort town, there's also a casino here. Along the casino is the **plage du Casino**. The large sandy beach **la plage de la Nartelle** is west of town.

If you're interested in visiting a picturesque village, head to **Grimaud**, 6 miles (10 km) west of St-Tropez. This village (pictured below) is one of France's "Villes Fleuries" (Flowered Villages) and it's truly lovely. The castle ruins (parts dating back to the 11th century) are high above the village and provide excellent vistas of St-Tropez Bay. During the day the town is filled with tourists, but at night it's a quiet place to dine and stroll.

The car-free town of **Port Grimaud** on the coast was constructed in the 1960s as a private resort complete with canals. Sort of a 1960s Venice in the South of France.

For fine views of the Bay of Pampelonne, head to **Ramatuelle**, 7 miles (12km) southwest of St-Tropez. Ramatuelle is built into the hills above the Bay of Pampelonne. It's surrounded by vineyards, and the village is enclosed by ramparts. Ancient stone houses line the narrow streets filled with boutiques and souvenir shops for the many day-trippers from St-Tropez. Lots of restaurants and small hotels.

Four miles (seven km) north of Ramatuelle is **Gassin**, another village worth a visit. Gassin is perched high up on a rock surrounded by vineyards. It's less commercial than nearby Ramatuelle. The village has ancient homes and winding streets. Its location is really the reason to visit. Not only can you see the Gulf of St-Tropez, but on a clear day, your view extends over the Maures Mountains.

If beach resorts are more to your liking, the area around the Gulf of St-Tropez offers many opportunities.

AROUND THE GULF OF ST-TROPEZ

Ste-Maxime To Fréjus

N98

Golfe de St-Tropez

Grimaud

Port Grimaud

La Foux

Plage des Graniers St-Tropez

Cap de St-Tropez

Cogolin

Route des Plages

Plage des Salins

Plage Tahiti

Pampelonne

Plage de Pampelonne

N98

Gassin

Ramatuelle

Coco Beach

La Croix-Valmer

Col de Collebasse L'Escalet

Cap Camarat

Le Mas de Gigaro

Baie de Bonporteau

Cavalaire-sur-Mer

Cap Taillat

To Hyères

Baie de Cavalaire

Cap Lardier

Fréjus is 20 miles (34 km) northeast of St-Tropez. Fréjus and nearby **St-Raphaël** seem to blend into each other as commercial beach resorts. Despite the town's bikini-wearing image, Fréjus's Old Town (**Vieille Ville**) has important Roman sights. The town was founded in 49 B.C. by Julius Caesar. You can view the remains of the **Théâtre Antique**, the 12,000-seat **Arènes** (an arena used today for the occasional bullfight and concert), and remaining arches of an **aqueduct**. Take a break from your tanning and visit these ruins.

Cité Épiscopale is an impressive fortified group of religious buildings in the Old Town. Outside the entry to the 12th-century cathedral is an octagonal baptistery from a 5th-century church that was located here. The cloisters feature galleries decorated with paintings from the 14th century. There's also a small archeology museum of Roman finds from the surrounding area. *Info: 58 rue de Fleury (in the Old Town). Tel. 04/94.51.26.30. Cloister, baptistery and museum are open 10am-1pm and 2pm-5pm (May-Aug 10am-6pm). Closed Mon. Cathedral is open daily 8:30am-noon and 2pm-6pm. Admission: Free (cathedral). Cloister, baptistery and museum: €6. www.cloitre-frejus.fr.*

Merging with Fréjus, **St-Raphaël** (1/2 mile [one km] southeast of Fréjus) is a modern beach resort. Unlike its neighbor, it has few historic sights. The Old Town (**Vieille Ville**) is the site of two churches, the 19th-century **Notre-Dame de la Victoire** and the 12th-century **Eglise des Templiers**.

Beside the Eglise des Templiers is the **Musée d'Archéologie Sous-Marine**, a museum dedicated to underwater archeology with ancient remains, a reconstructed Roman ship, early scuba systems, and access to a medieval church. *Info: rue des Templiers. Tel. 04/94.19.25.75. Open Mar-Oct 9am-12:30pm and 2pm-5pm. Closed Sun, Mon, and Tue morning. Nov-Feb 10am-12:30pm and 2pm-5pm. Closed Sun, Mon, Tue morning, and Sat afternoon. Admission: Free. www.musee-saint-raphael.com.*

You'll find a casino, hotels, and a promenade along the seafront. There are also five golf courses near St-Raphaël. First and foremost, this town is a beach town. Closest to town is **plage du Veillat**. A five-minute walk east of town is **plage Beau Rivage**. Even further east (about five miles) is **plage du Débarquement**. It was at this beach that the Allies landed in August of 1944 to begin their quest to liberate occupied France in World War II. In the other direction, about six miles west of town, is **plage de St-Ayguls**, a nude beach.

For stunning scenery, drive through the **Massif de l'Estérel** from St-Raphaël to La Napoule. This barren area of red volcanic rock provides strange and dramatic views. You can either travel north on route N7 or (for the more adventurous) along the coast on the **Corniche de l'Estérel** (route N98).

Looking for golf courses? Then visit **Mandelieu/La Napoule-Plage**. It's five miles (8 km) southwest of Cannes/20 miles (32 km) northeast of St- Raphaël. La Napoule is surrounded by the large resort town of **Mandelieu**. It was once a small fishing village on the Golfe de la Napoule. Its main sight is its **château**, a 14th-century fortress on the port. It was converted to a strange and interesting castle by eccentric American sculptor Henry Clews in the early 1900s. Now it's a museum of his works. Its garden is one of the finest in the Western French Riviera. *Info: Tel. 04/93.49.95.05. Open Feb-Oct 10am-6pm (four guided tours daily). Nov-Jan Mon-Fri 2pm-5pm (two guided tours daily), Sat and Sun 10am-5pm (three guided tours daily). Admission: €6. Admission to gardens only is €4. www.chateau-lanapoule.com.*

Cannes

Get glamorous in **Cannes**. It's 20 miles (33 km) southwest of Nice/45 miles (73 km) northeast of St-Tropez. You can reach Cannes from Nice by bus (#200, 1 3/4 hours) and by train (40 minutes).

This alluring resort with nearly perfect weather is best known for its international film festival (**Festival International du Film**) held every May, hosting countless film stars, over 4,000 journalists, and 1,500 other members of the media from around the world.

Head to **La Croisette**, a two-mile promenade on the waterfront. You'll see palm trees, polished yachts from every imaginable place in the world, incredible shops, ultra-luxury hotels, and some of the most interesting sun-worshippers in the world. At the beginning of La Croisette is the **Palais des Festivals** (Festivals Palace)/**Allée des Etoiles** (Walk of the Stars). Nicknamed "the bunker," the modern Palais des Festivals is the venue for the International Film Festival and many other events. Over 300 handprints are set in concrete on the Walk of Stars surrounding the Festival Hall. Also here is the Casino Croisette.

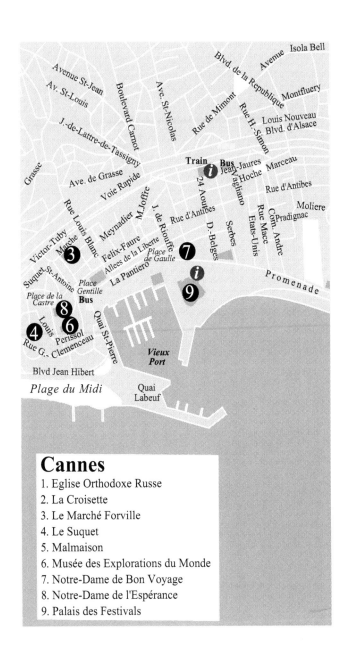

Cannes

1. Eglise Orthodoxe Russe
2. La Croisette
3. Le Marché Forville
4. Le Suquet
5. Malmaison
6. Musée des Explorations du Monde
7. Notre-Dame de Bon Voyage
8. Notre-Dame de l'Espérance
9. Palais des Festivals

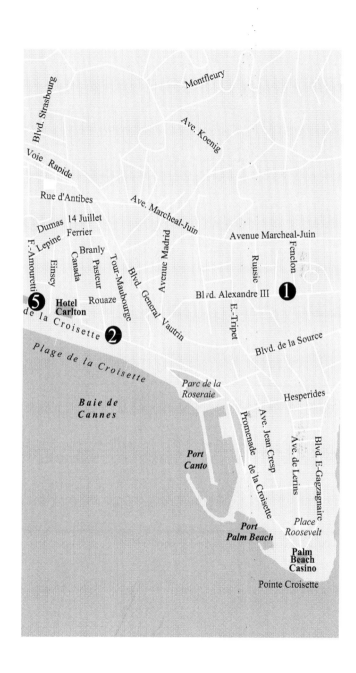

At number 47 La Croisette is **La Malmaison**. This 19th-century mansion hosts changing photography and modern-art exhibits. *Info: 47 La Croisette. Tel. 04/97.06.45.21. Admission: Depends on the exhibit.*

Just north of the Festivals Palace is **Notre-Dame de Bon Voyage**, a 19th-century Gothic-style church, where you can pray that you won't lose all your money at the nearby casinos. *Info: Square Mérimée. Open daily. Admission: Free.*

If you're looking for a place to take a break, there are plenty of cafés and restaurants along the waterfront.

The Old Town (**Le Suquet**) is on a hill on the west end of town. Narrow passageways lead to the **Tour du Suquet**, a 14th-century tower. *Info: Up rue St-Antoine from the waterfront (above quai St-Pierre).*

In the Old Town on the place de la Castre is **Notre-Dame de l'Espérance**, a 16th-century Gothic church. *Info: place de la Castre. Open daily. Admission: Free.*

At the top of Old Town is the **Musée des Explorations du Monde**. This museum is ambitious. It has a section on Mediterranean antiquities, a section of 19th-century paintings, and a section with sculpture, paintings and decorative arts from all over the world. *Info: In the Château de la Castre at the top of La Suquet. Tel. 04/89.82.26.26. Closed Mon. Open daily Jul and Aug. Admission: €6. www.cannes.com.*

If you're into shopping, there's something for everyone here. A few highlights of the phenomenal shopping in Cannes are:

• **Le Marché Forville**: a covered market not too far from Festival Hall featuring a flea market (Mon) and a produce and flower market (Tue through Sun). *www.marcheforville.com*

• **Galeries Lafayette**: a branch of this upscale French department store is located near the train station at 6 rue du Maréchal-Foch. *Closed most Sun*

• **La Croisette**: the promenade is loaded with designer boutiques (the Chanel boutique is at number 5!)

• **Rue d'Antibes**: a street (two blocks inland from the waterfront) filled with designer boutiques

• **CannOlive**: Provençal products, especially olive oils, at this long-standing shop at 16 & 20 rue Vénizelos. Closed Sun. *www.canolive.com.*

• **Rue Meynadier**: inland from the port, this pedestrian-only street is loaded with shops for most budgets .

While walking around town, you may stumble upon **Eglise Orthodoxe Russe**. It's so strange to see a Russian Orthodox Church in the South of France. The church, complete with onion dome, is dedicated to Michael the Archangel and was built by an expatriate Russian in the late 1800s. *Info: 40 boulevard Alexandre III. Open for services only. Admission: Free.*

Ready to take a break or just be a voyeur? Head to the beach! The **Plage de la Croisette** is along the promenade of the same name. For the most part, this is not a public beach. You must pay a fee (beginning at about €25) for use of a chaise longue, access to showers, food and drink service, an umbrella, and other amenities. For free beaches, try **plage Gazagnaire** to the east, or **plage du Midi** to the west.

Off the coast of Cannes are the **Iles de Lérins**. Traffic-free and tranquil, these islands can be reached by ferry from the Old Port (from €15). It takes 15 minutes to get to Ile Ste-Marguerite (filled with pine and eucalyptus trees, it's home to Fort

Royal, where "The Man in the Iron Mask" was imprisoned); and 30 minutes to Ile St-Honorat (home to a fortified abbey). *Info: From €15.50. www.cannes-ilesdelerins.com.*

If you're interested in abstract art, you can visit the **Espace de l'Art Concret** outside of Cannes in Mouans-Sartoux (in the castle), which houses a collection of 700 abstract works. *Info: Tel. 04/93.75.71.50. Open Oct-Jun Wed-Sun 1pm-6pm. Closed Mon and Tue. Jul and Aug daily 11am-7pm. Admission: €7. www.espacedelartconcret.fr.*

Golfers flock to the area around Cannes. Five miles (eight km) northeast of Cannes at 265 route dul Golf is the **Old Course Cannes**, where golfers can enjoy two stunning golf courses (18 holes and 9 holes). *Info: Tel. 04/92.97.32.00. Open daily. www.golfoldcourse.com.*

Cannes Sleeping & Eating
InterContinental Carlton €€€

The hotel in Cannes (and has been for years). Fashionable, plush and filled with celebrities during the film festival. Scenes from the Cary Grant and Grace Kelly movie *To Catch a Thief* were filmed here. Every amenity imaginable. Fantastic waterfront location with its own private beach.

Info: 58 blvd. De la Croisette. Tel. 04/93.06.40.06. V, MC, DC, AE. Restaurant, bar, gym, room service, AC, TV, telephone, CD player, minibar, in-room safe, hairdryer, WiFi. www.carlton-cannes.com.com. Closed for renovations until spring 2023.

Hôtel Splendid €€-€€€
We can't all stay at the Carlton, but we can perhaps afford the Splendid (especially in off-season). This 62-room, gleaming white hotel was renovated a few years ago, and has views overlooking the harbor. *Info: 4-6 rue Félix-Faure. Tel. 04/97.06.22.22. V, MC, AE. AC, TV, telephone, Internet, in-room safe, hairdryer, WiFi. www.splendid-hotel-cannes.fr.*

Hôtel Albert 1er €
Cannes is an expensive place to sleep. This mansion, in a mostly residential neighborhood, has been renovated and provides 12 small, clean, and comfortable rooms. Note that it is located uphill from the port and beaches. A good budget choice as rooms start at around €70. They also have two other boutique hotels in the city: **Le Romanesque** and **Jardin Croisette**. *Info: 68 ave. de Grasse. Tel. 04/93.39.24.04. V, MC, AE. AC, TV, WiFi. www. albert1er.com.*

La Meissounière €€
Mediterranean and Provençal dishes at this friendly restaurant. Try one of the pasta dishes like *tagliatelles au gorgonzola* (gorgonzola pasta) or the interesting *poêlée de St Jacques citron et soja* (scallops grilled with lemon and soy sauce). Whatever you do, don't forget to end you dinner with *profiterole au chocolat* (little cream puffs filled with ice cream and covered in chocolate sauce). Decent wine list features local producers. The three-course lunch is a good value at €23. *Info: 4 rue du 24 août (near the Gare Routière Bus Station). Tel. 04/93.38.37.76. Closed Sun and Mon. www.lameissouniere.com.*

La Table du Chef €€€
Unpretentious bistro (in a town of lots of pretentious restaurants) serving innovative French cuisine. There is no written menu, so you'll have to order the fixed menu. Chef Bruno Gensdarme worked at the famous Guy Savoy restaurant in Paris. He shops at local produce markets and then creates a nightly four-course menu. You won't be disappointed. *Info: 5 rue Jean Daumas (off of rue d'Antibes). Tel. 04/93.68.27.40. Closed Sun and Mon lunch and Tue lunch.*

Cannes Nightlife & Entertainment
After hitting the beach, head to **rue Félix Faure** where you will find many bars and clubs.

Carlton
The grand hotel bar at the InterContinental Carlton Hotel. Glamorous and expensive. *Info: 58 La Croisette. Tel. 04/93.06.40.06.*

Le Bâoli
Get out your wallet and enjoy cocktails at this restaurant/lounge and dance bar. *Info: Port Pierre Canto. Tel. 04/93.43.03.43. www.baolicannes.com.*

Casino Croisette
Part with your money at this popular casino facing the Palais des Festivals. *Info: 1 espace Lucien Barrière. Tel. 04/92.98.78.00. www.casinosbarriere.com.*

There are a few **gay and gay-friendly establishments** in Cannes: **Sauna Le-Neuf,** 8 Ch. De l'Industrie-Le Cannet. Tel. 06/17.94.29.24 (sauna with gay nights usually Mon-Wed and Sat evening). www.saunale9.com.
ParadX, 13 rue des Mimosas. Tel. 04/92.59.12.42 (cruise bar). paradxcannes.com.

Golfing in the French Riviera

Terre Blanche Hotel Spa Golf Resort €€€
Golfers will be in heaven at the two 18-hole courses. The resort, just south of Tourrettes and Fayence (19 miles [30 km] from Cannes and 35 miles [56 km] from Nice), offers everything a golf lover or non-golf lover could ever want. *Info: 3100 route de Bagnols-en-Forêt. Tel. 04/94.39.90.00. V, MC, DC, AE. Restaurant, bar, room service, outdoor pool, gym, AC, TV, telephone, CD/DVD player, minibar, hairdryer, safe, WiFi. www.terre-blanche.com.*

Around Cannes

The area around Cannes offers local-history museums, photography museums, art museums, and perfume museums.

We'll start in **Mougins**, five miles (eight km) north of Cannes. The area around Mougins has become a business center and home to thousands of French and international companies. The old village has been restored, is filled with flowers and galleries, and features the Porte Sarassine, a 12th-century gate.

Picasso and other artists came here in the 1960s, and Picasso died here in 1973. His final home is in the priory next door to the **Chapelle Notre-Dame de Vie**, an ancient church overlooking the Bay of Cannes. Note that Picasso's former home is privately owned, and the chapel is only open for services. *Info: It's located off of route D35 (1 mile [1.5 km] southeast of town).*

The **Centre de la Photographie de Mougins** is located in a former presbytery and is filled with photography equipment and photos (some of Picasso during his life in Mougins). The center has three changing exhibits each year. *Info: Near the Porte Sarassine at 43 rue de l'Eglise. Tel. 04/22.21.52.12. Open Apr-Oct 11am-8pm. Closed Tue. Nov-Mar 1pm-6pm. Closed Mon and Tue. Admission: €2. centrephotographiemougins.com.*

Grasse is 10 miles (17 km) northwest of Cannes/14 miles (22 km) northwest of Antibes/26 miles (42 km) southwest of Nice. Once a famous resort destination (the likes of Queen Victoria used to come here), today Grasse is a modern town and the headquarters of some of the world's best-known and largest perfume manufacturers. The majority of all perfume sold in the world contains essences from Grasse. The city's three largest perfume makers have free guided tours: Fragonard at 20 boulevard Fragonard, Molinard at 60 boulevard Victor-Hugo, and Galimard at 73 route de Cannes (two miles [three km] south of the center of town). Lots of signs point the way to these factories. The Vieille Ville (Old Town) has narrow, steep streets without the glitz of coastal old towns.

Grasse has three very different museums:

Musée Fragonard
Fragonard was one of France's distinguished 18th-century artists. This museum, in the town center, honors this native son of Grasse and showcases his paintings. *Info: 14 rue Jean Ossola. Tel. 04/93.36.02.07. Currently closed for renovations. Admission: Free.*

Le Musée du Parfum à Grasse will tell you everything you wanted to know about perfume and its 4,000-year history. Put your nose to the test at one exhibit by trying to identify different fragrances. *Info: 20 blvd. Fragonard (3rd floor). Tel. 04/93.36.44.65. Open daily 9am-6pm. Admission: Free.*

You'll find local paintings, archeological finds, household items and pottery at the **Musée d'Art et d'Histoire de Provence** (Museum of Art and History of Provence). It's located in a mansion built in 1772. *Info: 2 rue Mirabeau. Tel. 04/93.36.80.20. Open May-Sep 10am-7pm (Oct-Apr until 6pm). Admission: €2.*

Grasse Sleeping & Eating
La Bastide St-Antoine €€€
A 200-year-old farmhouse and inn (the Rolling Stones once stayed here) is the site of an award-winning restaurant (€€€). There are nine luxury rooms and seven suites. *Info: 48 avenue Henri-Dunant. Tel. 04/93.70.94.94. V, MC, DC, AE. AC, TV, telephone, minibar, in-room safe, hairdryer, WiFi. www.jacques-chibois.com.*

If you're up for more touring, you can visit **Vallauris/Golfe-Juan**. It's four miles (six km) west of Antibes/four miles (six km) northeast of Cannes.

Vallauris is a working-class-town and has long been a center for the production of pottery and ceramics. Most come here to visit the museum dedicated to the works of Picasso. On the coast is the port of **Golfe-Juan**. It was here in 1815 that Napoléon arrived after being exiled to the island of Elba in his attempt to return to power. Today it's a family beach resort.

Picasso lived in this town in the 1940s and devoted much of his time to creating pottery. The **Musée National Picasso (La Guerre et La Paix)** is located in the 16th-century Château de Vallauris. Two of Picasso's paintings (*La Paix* [Peace] and *La Guerre* [War]) decorate the walls. Also here are the **Musée de la Céramique Moderne**, exhibiting Picasso and others' ceramic works, and **Musée Magnelli**, devoted to the works of Italian abstract artist Alberto Magnelli. *Info: place de la Libération. Tel. 04/93.64.71.83. Open daily 10am-12:15pm and 2pm-5pm. Admission: €6. www.musee-picasso-vallauris.fr.*

If you'd like to take a detour from the coast and its resorts, you can drive 110 miles (176 km) along the **Route Napoléon** from Grasse (near the coast) to Sisteron, mainly on route N85. Napoléon Bonaparte abdicated in April, 1814, and fled to the island of Elba. Nearly a year later, he landed near Cannes. From Cannes, Napoléon and 1,200 men followed small trails and mule tracks through the hills. Traveling its entirety can take up to 15 hours. Plaques commemorating his return are found along this panoramic drive. **Sisteron** is the northern gateway to Provence. It's crowned by a 14th-century fortified citadel. On your way up to the citadel is the 12th-century church of **Notre-Dame des Pommiers**. You'll find incredible views of the Durance River valley from the citadel after you climb up Sisteron's tiny winding streets, covered alleys and steep stairways. The last inhabitants of the citadel were the Nazis in 1944, who used it as a prison and military base.

Antibes

Antibes is an ancient town with 17th-century ramparts and a fortress wall dropping into the sea. It's nine miles (15 km) southeast of Nice/seven miles (11 km) northeast of Cannes. You can reach Antibes from the airport in Nice by bus (#200, 1.5 hours) and by train (30 minutes). *www.sncf-connect.com.*

The streets of its Old Town (**Vieil Antibes**) are lined with Italianate buildings with red-tile roofs. High over the water is the medieval castle, the **Château Grimaldi**. It's also a major tourist destination, with a sandy beach, boutiques, and cafés. **Port Vauban Harbor** is packed with some of the largest yachts in the world.

Begin your day in Antibes at the harborside car park along avenue de Verdun (the main street along the harbor).

Pass through the arched gateway (the **Porte Marine**). The rampart walls date back to the 17th century when Antibes was the last town before the Italian border. You'll now be in the Old Town (**Vieil Antibes**) on rue Aubernon lined with Italianate buildings.

If you're looking to take a break at a café, head to the tree-lined **Place Nationale** on rue de la République.

The heart of Antibes is the 19th-century canopy of the **Marché Provençal** (Provence Market). Everything from flowers to produce to crafts to beachwear can be found here.

In the Old Town, at place de la Cathédrale, is the **Eglise de l'Immaculée-Conception** (Church of the Immaculate Conception). Its bell tower dates back to the 11th century. You enter through elaborate walnut doors carved in the early 1700s. Inside you can view its Baroque painted altars. *Info: 1 rue Saint-Esprit. Tel. 04/93.34.80.10. Open daily. Admission: Free.*

Across the street from the cathedral is the famous **Musée Picasso**. Picasso spent a very productive year here in the early 1940s at the Château Grimaldi. He gave the museum 300 works (ceramics, drawings, paintings, lithographs, tapestries, sculptures, and oils on paper). There are works by other artists, too, including Miró and Calder. *Info: place du Château (in the Château Grimaldi). Tel. 04/92.90.54.20. Open Tue-Sun mid-Sep to mid-Jun 10am-1pm and 2pm-6pm, mid-Jun to mid-Sep 10am-6pm. Closed Mon. Admission: €8.*

If you're interested in catching some rays, join the sunbathers at the public beach, **plage de la Gravette**.

The archeology museum **Musée d'Histoire et d'Archéologie** is located in the fortress Bastion-St-André. It's filled with finds from the area dating back to the Greeks, who settled here in the 4th-century B.C. *Info: Tel. 04/93.95.85.98. Open Tue-Sun 10am-12:30pm and 2pm-6pm. Closed Mon. Admission: €3.*

Whales, sharks, dolphins, sea lions, waterslides, miniature golf, petting zoo...you get the picture. Children will love **Marineland**. *Info: Hwy A8 towards Nice, exit Antibes (No. 44) toward S. Antipolis, then follow the signs to Marineland. Tel. 04/93.33.49.49. Admission: €39 adults, €32 children (under 13). www.marineland.fr.*

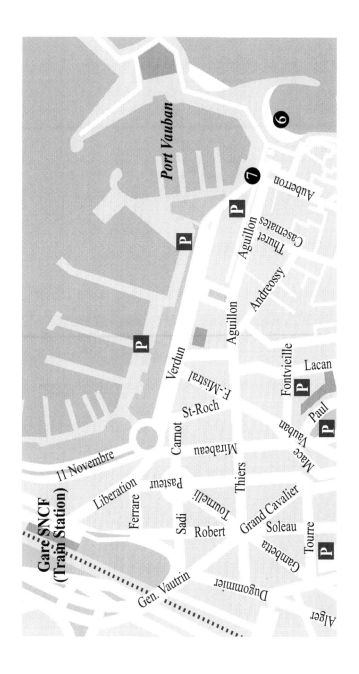

Antibes

1. Eglise de l'Immaculée-Conception
2. Marché Provençal
3. Musée d'Histoire et d'Archéologie
4. Musée Picasso
5. Place Nationale
6. Plage de la Gravette
7. Porte Marine

You may want to spend some time in **Cap d' Antibes**, just one mile (two km) south of Antibes. Since the 19th century, this peninsula has been home to luxury villas shaded by massive pines and protected by privacy gates.

One of the world's most glamorous hotels (**Hôtel du Cap-Eden Roc**) is located here. There are fabulous views from the lighthouse (Phare de la Garoupe) next to the 16th-century chapel of Notre-Dame-de-la-Garoupe.

If you're interested in subtropical plants and trees, head to the **Jardin Thuret**. Thuret was the man responsible for introducing the palm tree to this area. This garden features over 1,600 species of exotic trees and shrubs *Info: boulevard du Cap. Tel. 04/92.38.64.70. Open 8:30am-5:30pm (8am-6pm in summer). Closed weekends. Admission: Free.*

Antibes/Cap d'Antibes Sleeping & Eating

Hôtel du Cap-Eden Roc €€€
Simply one of the world's most stylish hotels. It's so exclusive that it didn't take credit cards until a few years ago. The swimming pool, dug into solid rock, is spectacular. It's surrounded by nine acres of lush gardens. *Info: Blvd. J.F.-Kennedy in Cap d'Antibes. Tel. 04/93.61.39.01. Restaurant, bar, outdoor pool, tennis courts, AC, TV, telephone, minibar, safe, hairdryer, WiFi. www.oetkercollection.com.*

Hôtel La Jabotte €€
A small gem of a hotel (really more like a bed and breakfast) for the cost, hidden down an alley in Cap d'Antibes. Lovely patio garden, basic accommodations and friendly owners. *Info: 13 ave. Max-Maurey. Tel. 04/93.61.45.89. V, MC. AC, TV, telephone. WiFi available. www.jabotte.com.*

Les Vieux Murs €€€
This candlelit restaurant/tavern is located in a vaulted room inside the town walls near the Musée Picasso. Great views of the sea. Local seafood is the specialty. Large selection of wines from Provence. *Info: 25 promenade Amiral-de-Grasse. Tel. 04/93.34.06.73. Closed Sun dinner and Mon. www.lesvieuxmurs.com.*

A Memorable Walk at Sunset

Begin this phenomenal walk at the plage de la Garoupe, the cape's beach. You can park at the public parking lot. At the end of the beach and parking lot is the **Sentier du Littoral**. This stone path (at times dirt) has steps etched into the rocky coastline. Although it winds its way around the entire cape, remember that you need to return to your car. It's for the adventurous and at times the waves can make the path slippery and dangerous. The total walk is about two hours.

Angelo's by Le Milano €€

Small, intimate restaurant with an open kitchen. Dishes are beautifully presented. Try one of the excellent Italian dishes offered such as *risotto aux artichauts et safran* (artichoke and saffron risotto) or *tagliolini aux champignons* (tagliolini pasta with mushrooms). These are some of the vegetarian options, but you can order fish or meat. *Info: 2 rue de la Tourrague (near the intersection of cours Masséna). Tel. 04/89.68.62.18. Closed Wed.*

Le Brûlot €-€€

Crowded, hectic bistro one street inland from the open-air market, serving authentic Provençal fare, Italian dishes, and pizza cooked in a wood oven. *Info: Le Brûlot: 3 rue Frédéric-Isnard (off of rue Clemenceau). Tel. 04/93.34.17.76. Closed Sun. www.brulot.fr.*

Juan-les-Pins is three miles (five km) southwest of Antibes.

Modern, crowded, sexy, and a little bit naughty. **Juan-les-Pins**, developed in the 1920s, is known for its nightlife and tends to draw a younger crowd than nearby Antibes. You can take a break from visiting the clubs at Eden Casino. While most of the coast has pebble beaches, the town's three public beaches, **plage de Juan-les-Pins, plage de la Salis**, and **plage de la Garoupe**, are sandy. It hosts a world-renowned jazz festival every July. *Info: www.antibes-juanlespins.com.*

Around Antibes
Pottery, art, and unbelievable scenery are in store for you in the area around Antibes. Begin in **Biot**, four miles (six km) northwest of Antibes. This 16th-century hilltop village is known for its pottery, ceramics, and glassblowing. Around the main square, the **place des Arcades**, are the ancient gateways and the **Eglise de Biot** with its elaborately decorated 15th-century altar screens.

There are many shops here where you can buy pottery, ceramics, and decorative glassware, and most of them are near the place des Arcades. You can watch glassblowers and purchase glassware at **Verreries de Biot** at 5 chemin des Combes on the edge of town. Closed part of Jan. *www.verreriebiot.com.*

The **Musée d'Histoire Locale et de Céramique Biotoise** chronicles the importance of ceramics, pottery and glassblowing in local history. *Info: place de la Chapelle/9 rue St-Sébastien. Tel. 04/93.65.54.54. www.musee-de-biot.fr. Closed Mon and Tue. Admission: €4.*

You may also want to visit the **Musée National Fernand-Léger** on the east end of the village. Léger was a French cubist painter who died in 1955. This national museum, with its very colorful exterior, houses over 300 of his works. *Info: 255 Chemin du Val de Pôme (on the east end of the village). Tel. 04/93.53.87.20. Open Nov-Apr 10am-5pm (May-Oct to 6pm). Closed Tue. Admission: €6. musees-nationaux-alpesmaritimes.fr/fleger/.*

Inland is the incredible village of **Gourdon**, 9 miles (14 km) north of Grasse.

This clifftop village stands dramatically on limestone overlooking the Loup River Valley. It's worth the drive up the winding roads. The town offers spectacular views (and we do mean spectacular) of both the coast and the river canyon. The Loup River has cut its way through the limestone to create a series of rapids and waterfalls, and the river canyon is one of the most accessible in the area.

You can walk from town down the adventurous **chemin du Paradis**. The city is popular with hikers, rafters, and trout fishermen. It's an ancient feudal town where you can visit the tranquil gardens of **Gourdon Castle**.

If you want to check out one more village near Antibes, head to the lovely town of **Tourrettes-sur-Loup**. It's 18 miles (29 km) west of Nice/four miles (six km) west of Vence.

This village with its three towers sits on a cliff overlooking the Loup River Valley. The walls of the outer buildings of the village also serve as ramparts. It's a center for the cultivation of violets, and you'll see them everywhere. The **Old Town** is lovely and worth a stroll. You can visit the **Chapelle St-Jean** next to **Roman ruins**. The town is loaded with interesting galleries selling their crafts and plenty of candy shops, some of them selling sugar candy made with local violets (we told you they were everywhere).

Further Afield

Join the crowds in **St-Paul-de-Vence**, 19 miles (31 km) north of Nice. *See photo page 97.*

Said to be the most visited village in France, **St-Paul** is crowded with day-trippers from the coastal resort towns and Nice. What makes it so popular is its walled, beautifully preserved Old Town of stone houses dating back to the 16th and 17th centuries. You can walk down the car-free main street (**Grande Rue**) past its souvenir shops and art galleries, up to the art-filled **La Collégiale de la Conversion de St-Paul** (an early Gothic church), and visit the **Musée d'Histoire Locale (Local History Museum)**.

Outside the town walls on the hilltop (a 15-minute uphill walk from town or access by car) is the **Fondation Maeght**. Even those not interested in modern art can appreciate this world-famous venue. Glass walls let you take in the pine-shaded gardens and terraces while you view changing exhibits of works by such artists as Chagall, Matisse, Kandinsky, Calder, and Miró. This private museum was established in the 1960s by art dealer Aimé Maeght, and its unique architecture alone is worth a visit. *Info: Outside the town walls on the hilltop (a 15-minute uphill walk from town or access by car). Tel. 04/93.32.81.63. Open daily 10am-6pm (July and Aug until 7pm). Admission: €16. www.fondation-maeght.com.*

St-Paul-de-Vence Sleeping & Eating

Auberge Le Hameau €€€

This former farmhouse on the outskirts of town provides an oh, so Riviera experience. Some of the 17 rooms and suites have terraces facing the lovely outdoor pool; others have views of St-Paul or the Mediterranean Sea. Rooms are decorated with Provençal furniture. *Info: 528 Route de la Colle/D107 (a little less than one mile from St-Paul in the direction of Colle). Tel. 04/83.39.95.94. V, MC. Bar, outdoor pool, AC, TV, gym, telephone, minibar, hairdryer, safe, WiFi. Closed mid-Nov to mid-Feb. www.le-hameau.com.*

La Colombe d'Or €€€
This exclusive, family-run 26-room villa is just 12 miles from
Nice, and is surrounded by cypress trees. Beautiful outdoor
pool. Cozy rooms decorated with ceramic tile. Most come
here for its restaurant, with art of such notables as Picasso and
Utrillo on the walls. *Info: 1 place du Général-de-Gaulle. Tel.
04/93.32.80.02. V, MC, DC, AE. Restaurant, bar, outdoor pool,
AC, TV, telephone, minibar, hairdryer, safe, WiFi. Closed Nov and
Dec. www.la-colombe-dor.com.*

Le Tilleul €€
Located on the town's ramparts, this restaurant is a great place
to relax for breakfast, lunch, or dinner. The all-French wine
list includes many selections by the glass. Sip your wine while
sitting under the large lime tree or dine on modern French cuisine in the attractive indoor dining area. Try the *poulet fermier
cuisiné au lait de coco et curry* (free-range chicken in a coconut
milk and curry sauce). If you're missing Mexican beer, they also
serve Corona! *Info: place du Tilleul. Tel. 04/93.32.80.36. Open
daily in season. www.restaurant-letilleul.com.*

Just two miles (four km) north of St-Paul-de-Vence is the city
of **Vence**.

Vence is a modern commercial town and most travelers head to
its walled Old Town (**Cité Historique**). Most of the renovated
Old Town dates back to the 15th century. Sections of the origi-
nal walls survive and there are five gates (*portes*) that remain.

Inside these gates are the 13th-century watchtower of the
Château de Villeneuve on **place du Frêne** (which takes its name
from the ancient ash tree (*frêne*) here), the **place du Peyra** (with
its lovely fountains), and the **place Clemenceau** (dominated by
the City Hall). On **place Godeau** is the **Cathédrale de la Na-
tivité de la Vierge** (Cathedral of the Birth of the Virgin), with
portions dating back to the 10th century.

On the northern outskirts of town is the **Chapelle du Ro-saire** (Chapel of the Rosary). At the age of 77, in thanks to a Dominican nun (and sometimes model!) who nursed him back to health, Matisse designed and decorated this small chapel on the northern outskirts of town. Its white walls are highlighted with blue-and-green stained-glass windows and black-and-white Stations of the Cross. The admission includes entry to a museum that chronicles the design and construction of the chapel. *Info: 466 avenue Henri-Matisse. Tel. 04/93.58.03.26. Open Mar-Oct Wed-Sat 2pm-5:30pm, Thu-Fri 10am-11:30am and 2pm-5:30pm. Nov-Feb Wed-Sat 2pm-4:30pm and Tue, Thu, Fri 10am-noon and 2pm-5pm. Admission: €7. www.chapellematisse.fr.*

Vence Eating
La Farigoule €€-€€€
Classic Provençal cuisine with indoor and outdoor dining. The Provençal dish *pissaladière* (a pizza-like tart with onions, black olives and purée of anchovies and sardines) is a specialty here. *Info: 15 rue Henri-Isnard (in the Old Town). Tel. 04/93.58.01.27. Closed Mon andTue.www.lafarigoule-vence.fr.*

If you're up for more touring, you can visit **Cagnes-sur-Mer**, 4 miles (6 km) south of St-Paul-de-Vence/13 miles (21 km) northeast of Cannes.

Cagnes-sur-Mer is really three different places. At the sea is the former fishing village and now modern beach resort of **Cros-de-Cagnes** (with a pebble beach). Inland is the modern town of **Cagnes-Ville**, and up the hill is the beautiful fortified medieval village of **Haut-de-Cagnes**.

In **Haut-de-Cagnes**, you'll find the **Château de Cagne**. This Grimaldi fortress was built in the early 1300s. Inside its walls is an elegant palace dating back to 1602. It houses the museum of modern Mediterranean art and a museum dedicated to the history of the olive tree. *Info: place Grimaldi. Tel. 04/93.02.47.30. Closed Tue. Admission: €4.*

Admirers of Renoir should visit the **Musée Renoir**, located in the former home of the artist. It has been renovated and restored to how it was when he died in 1919. The museum sits in the middle of olive groves just east of the Old Town. Eleven of his paintings and the largest collection of his sculpture are here, along with those of his contemporaries. *Info: avenue des Collettes (brown signs mark the way). Tel. 04/93.20.61.07. Open Jun-Sep Wed-Mon 10am-1pm and 2pm-6pm, Oct-Mar 10am-noon and 2pm-5pm, Apr-May 10am-noon and 2pm-6pm. Closed Tue. Admission: €6. www.cagnes-sur-mer.fr.*

Haut-de-Cagnes Sleeping & Eating
Le Grimaldi €€
Indoor and outdoor dining on the Old Town square at this family-owned restaurant serving local specialties. Try the *lapin* (rabbit). The small inn (€€) features five comfortable rooms. *Info: 6 place du Château in Haut-de-Cagnes. Tel. 04/93.08.67.12. Open Oct-Mar. Inn: V, MC, AE. TV, AC, WiFi. Restaurant Closed Mon and Tue. www.hotelgrimaldi.com.*

6. PRACTICAL MATTERS

GETTING TO THE FRENCH RIVIERA

Airport/Arrival

The **Nice-Côte d'Azur Airport** is on a peninsula 20 minutes west of the central city of Nice. A taxi into town costs at least €32. Rideshare to central Nice costs around €20.

Trams run seven days a week from 5am until midnight. On weekdays, trams run every five minutes from 7:30am to 8:00pm. On Saturdays, trams arrive every six minutes between 7:00am and 8:00pm. Sunday trams run every nine minutes between 8:00am and 9:00pm. For €1.50, a single pass has unlimited transfers on buses or trams within 74 minutes of validation (one direction only). Bus tickets may be purchased from the driver, but tram tickets must be purchased before boarding at vending machines at the stop. The machines only take credit cards with chips or Euro coins. A 10-ride pass cost €10 (€1 per ride) and may be used by more than one person on the same trip.

All major car-rental companies are represented at the airport.

You can also fly to Paris and then take a train south (see next page).

GETTING AROUND

Cars & Driving

Renting a car and driving is the best way to see the areas covered in this book. Note that parking can be difficult in high season. Driving within major cities can be a headache. Gas is very expensive, but a mitigating factor is that the cars are smaller and more energy-efficient. You will either take a ticket when you get on the autoroute and pay (look for the signs that say *péage*) when you get off, or pay as you go.

Kilometers-Miles

One kilometer = 0.62 miles.
To convert miles to kilometers, multiply by 1.61.
So, 1 mile = 1.61 kilometers.

In order of fastest to slowest, routes are as follows: A means autoroute, N means national route, and D means departmental route. Be prepared for narrow roads, high speeds and hairpin turns.

Train & Bus Travel

SNCF is the rail system for France. TGV trains are fast-speed trains that travel at up to 220 mph.

The trip on the TGV from Paris to Nice is 6 hours, as not all of the trip is high-speed. *Info: www.sncf.com.*

There's a coastal rail line that runs from Ventimiglia on the Italian border (Vintimille in French) to Marseille. There are trains that run nearly every hour on this line. Stops on this scenic train ride include: Menton, Cap-Martin, Monaco, Èze-sur-Mer (not to be confused with hilltop Èze), Beaulieu, St-Jean-Cap-Ferrat, Villefranche-sur-Mer, Nice, Antibes and Cannes. You must validate (*composter*) your ticket at a machine (watch locals do it) before you get on a SNCF train.

Regional bus service is good, but is limited on Sundays. Train service is in most cases faster, but bus service is generally cheaper.

Holidays
• New Year's: January 1
• Easter
• Ascension (40 days after Easter)
• Pentecost (seventh Sunday after Easter)

- May Day: May 1
- Victory in Europe: May 8
- Bastille Day: July 14
- Assumption of the Virgin Mary: August 15
- All Saints': November 1
- Armistice: November 11
- Christmas: December 25

BASIC INFORMATION

Banking & Changing Money

The euro (€) is the currency of France and most of Europe. Before you leave for France, it's a good idea to get some euros. It makes your arrival a lot easier. Call your credit-card company or bank before you leave to tell them that you'll be using your ATM or credit card outside the country. Many have automatic controls that can "freeze" your account if the computer program determines that there are charges outside your normal area. ATMs (with fees, of course) are the easiest way to change money in France. You'll find them everywhere. You can still get traveler's checks, but why bother? Especially since many establishments will not take them for fear of counterfeit checks. Note that many establishments no longer accept cash and you must pay with a card. This is a growing trend throughout Europe.

Business Hours

Many attractions and offices in the French Riviera close at noon and reopen and hour or two later.

Climate & Weather

Expect hot and dry weather except for periods of heavy rain in spring. November, December and January can be quite cold and wet, with temperatures dipping to lows in the upper 30s. The average high temperature in July and August is 84 degrees. The Mistral wind blows 30 to 60 miles per hour about 100 days of the year in Provence. It begins above the Alps and Massif Central Mountains, gaining speed as it heads south toward the Mediterranean Sea. Le Mistral is followed by clear skies.

Consulates & Embassies
• US Consulate, Marseille: place Varian Fry, Tel. 01/43.12.48.85 (note that the consultae in Nice is now closed)
• Canadian Consulate, Nice: 10 rue Lamartine, Tel. 04/93.92.93.22
• UK Consulate, Marseille: 10 place de la Joliette, Tel. 04/91.15.72.10.

Electricity
The electrical current in France is 220 volts as opposed to 110 volts found at home. Don't fry your electric razor, hairdryer, or laptop. You'll need a converter and an adapter. Most laptops don't require a converter, but why are you bringing them on vacation anyway?

Emergencies & Safety
Don't wear a fanny pack; it's a sign that you're a tourist and an easy target (especially in crowded tourist areas). Avoid wearing expensive jewelry. Don't leave valuables in your car. In case of an emergency, dial 112. Pharmacies can refer you to a doctor.

Insurance
Check with your health-care provider. Most policies don't cover you overseas. If that's the case, you may want to obtain medical insurance. Given the uncertainties in today's world, you may also want to purchase trip-cancellation insurance. Make sure that your policy covers sickness, disasters, bankruptcy, and State Department travel restrictions and warnings. In other words, read the fine print! *Info: www.insuremytrip.com* for insurance coverage.

Internet Access/WiFi
Cyber cafés seem to pop up everywhere (and go out of business quickly). You shouldn't have difficulty finding a place to e-mail home. Remember that French keyboards are different than those found in the U.S. and Canada. WiFi is now readily available at hotels and cafes. To access the Internet, the cheaper

option is to use free WiFi. Don't incur huge charges by incurring data roaming charges.

If you want to use your smartphone and not worry about data or voice charges, simply turn off both data and voice roaming or place your phone in "Airport Mode." When you use WiFi exclusively, you can stay connected and avoid unnecessary charges.

Language

Please, make the effort to speak a little French. It will get you a long way, even if all you can say is Parlez-vous anglais? (*par-lay voo ahn-glay*): Do you speak English? Gone are the days when the French were only interested in correcting your French. There's a list of helpful French phrases in this book.

Packing

Never pack prescription drugs, eyeglasses, or valuables. Carry them on. Oh, and by the way, pack light. Don't ruin your trip by having to lug around huge suitcases. Before you leave home, make copies of your passport, airline tickets, and confirmation of hotel reservations. You should also make a list of your credit-card numbers and the telephone numbers for your credit-card companies. If you lose any of them (or they're stolen), you can call someone at home and have them provide the information to you. You should also pack copies of these documents separate from the originals.

Passport Regulations

You'll need a valid passport to enter France. If you're staying more than 90 days, you must obtain a visa. Canadians don't need visas. Canadians can bring back C$750 each year if they have been gone for 7 days or more.

US citizens who have been away more than 48 hours can bring home $800 of merchandise duty-free every 30 days. *Info: go to help.cbp.gov.*

Postal Services

Post offices – PTT – are found in nearly every town. You'll recognize them by their yellow La Poste signs. They're generally open weekdays from 8am-7pm and Saturdays from 8am until noon. Some post offices, especially those in smaller towns, close for an hour or two in the middle of the day.

Rest Rooms

There aren't a lot of public rest rooms. If you need to go, your best bet is to head (no pun intended) to the nearest café or brasserie. It's considered good manners to purchase something if you use the rest room. Don't be shocked to walk into a rest room and find two porcelain footprints and a hole in the floor. These old "Turkish toilets" still exist (but are rare). Hope you have strong thighs!

Taxes

Hotel and restaurant prices are required by law to include taxes and service charges. Value Added Tax (VAT or TVA in France) is nearly 20% (higher on luxury goods). The VAT is included in the price of goods (except services such as restaurants). Foreigners are entitled to a refund and must fill out a refund form. When you make your purchase, you should ask for the form and instructions if you're purchasing €175 or more in one place and in one day (no combining). Yes, it can be a hassle. Info: Check out www.globalblue.com for the latest information on refunds (and help for a fee).

Telephone

• Country code for France is 33
• Area code for Provence and the French Riviera is 04
• Calls beginning with 0800 are toll-free
• Calling France from the U.S. and Canada: dial 011-33-4 plus the eight-digit local number. You drop the 0 in the area code
• Calling the U.S. or Canada from France: dial 00 (wait for the tone), dial 1 plus the area code and local number
• Calling within Provence and the French Riviera: dial 04 and the eight-digit local number.

You can also purchase an international prepaid SIM card *www.simoptions.com.*

A great way to stay in touch and save money is to rent an international cell phone. One provider is www.cellhire.com. Some cell phones purchased in the U.S. do not work in Europe. If you're a frequent visitor to Europe, you may want to purchase a cell phone (for about $50) from www.mobal.com. You'll get an international telephone number, and pay for calls by the minute. Many smartphones work in Europe. Contact your provider to access a global plan for the time period you will be in Europe. When in Europe, minimize roaming charges by using WiFi. For more information on avoiding charges on your smartphone while in Europe, see the "Internet Access" section of this chapter above.

Time
When it's noon in New York City, it's 6pm in the French Riviera. For hours of events or schedules, the French use the 24-hour clock. So 6am is 06h00 and 1pm is 13h00.

Tipping
See the Restaurants section, beginning on page 107, for tipping in restaurants. Other tips: up to 5% for taxi drivers, €1 for room service, €1.50 per bag to the hotel porter, €1.50 per day for maid service and €0.50 to bathroom attendants.

Tourist Information
Nearly every town in this book has a helpful tourist-information center. Tourist offices in Nice sell money-saving museum passes. *See page 22.*

Water
Tap water is safe in France. Occasionally, you'll find *non potable* signs in rest rooms. This means that the water is not safe for drinking.

Websites

For the French Government Tourist Office go to www.france.com. For the US State Department Foreign Entry Requirements go to www.state.gov.

Hotels & Restaurants
Hotels

We've listed hotels throughout the French Riviera in this book. We've also included some wonderful bed-and-breakfast establishments and farmhouses that have been converted into inns and hotels.

Hotel Prices in this Book
Prices for two people in a double room:

- Expensive (over €200): €€€
- Moderate (€100-200): €€
- Inexpensive (under €100): €

In addition to the lodgings in this book, you could also stay at one of the many *gîtes* (country homes that can be rented by travelers, usually by the week). In an effort to preserve these country homes, the French government offers subsidies to rehabilitate them and a program to market them for rental. There are thousands of these homes in France, from luxury to budget. For information on this great way to experience France, especially if traveling as a family or group, visit www.gite.com or www.gites-de-france.fr/eng.

Restaurants

You've come to France in part to enjoy the best cuisine in the world, right? You will not be disappointed. We have selected the best restaurants within different price ranges, and we also give you some tips to help you save money and still eat a meal that will be memorable and fantastique in every way!

Restaurant Prices in this Book
Restaurant prices in this book are for a main course.

- Expensive: (over €20) €€€
- Moderate: (€10-20) €€
- Inexpensive: (under €10) €

There's no need to spend a lot of money in the French Riviera to eat well. Of course it hurts when the dollar is weaker than the euro, but there are all kinds of fabulous foods to be had inexpensively.

Eat at a neighborhood restaurant or bistro. You'll always know the price of a meal before entering, as almost all restaurants post the menu and prices in the window. Never order anything whose price is not known in advance. If you see *selon grosseur* (sometimes abbreviated as s/g) this means that you're paying by weight, which can be extremely expensive.

Delis and food stores can provide cheap and wonderful meals. Buy some cheese, bread, wine and other snacks and have a picnic. In fact, no matter what, you should go into a *boulangerie* and buy a baguette at least once. Remember to pack a corkscrew and eating utensils when you leave.

Lunch, even at the most expensive restaurants listed in this guide, always has a lower fixed price. So have lunch as your main meal. Many French do.

Restaurants and bistros that have menus written in English (especially those near tourist attractions) are almost always more expensive than neighborhood restaurants and bistros.

Street vendors in larger towns generally sell inexpensive and terrific food; you'll find excellent hot dogs, crêpes and roast-chicken sandwiches.

For the cost of a cup of coffee or a drink, you can linger at a café and watch the world pass you by for as long as you want. It's one of France's greatest bargains.

The bill in a restaurant is called *l'addition* ... but the bill in a bar is called *le compte* or *la note*. Confused? It's easier if you just make a scribbling motion with your fingers on the palm of your hand.

A service charge is almost always added to your bill. Depending on the service, it's *sometimes* appropriate to leave up to 5%. Most locals round up to the next euro and it's okay if that is what you do, too. Travelers from the U.S. sometimes have trouble *not* tipping. Remember, you do not have to tip.

The menu will usually note that service is included (*service compris*). Sometimes this is abbreviated with the letters s.c. The letters s.n.c. stand for *service non compris*; this means that the service is not included in the price, and you must leave a tip. This is extremely rare. You'll sometimes find *couvert* or cover charge on your menu (a small charge just for placing your butt at the table).

A menu is a fixed-price meal, not that piece of paper listing the food items. If you want what we consider a menu, you need to ask for *la carte*. The menu is almost always posted on the front of the restaurant so you know what you're getting into, both foodwise and pricewise, before you enter.

Mealtimes
Lunch is served from around 1pm and dinner from around 8pm. Make reservations!

Dogs Allowed!
The French really love their dogs. In restaurants, it's not uncommon to find several dogs under tables, or even on their own chairs.

ESSENTIAL FRENCH PHRASES

please, *s'il vous plait* (seel voo *play*)
thank you, *merci* (*mair* see)
yes, *oui* (wee)
no, *non* (nohn)
good morning, *bonjour* (bohn *jhoor*)
good afternoon, *bonjour* (bohn *jhoor*)
good evening, *bonsoir* (bohn *swahr*)
goodbye, *au revoir* (o ruh *vwahr*)
sorry/excuse me, *pardon* (pahr-*dohn*)
you are welcome, *de rien* (duh ree *ehn*)

do you speak English?, *parlez-vous anglais?* (par lay voo ahn *glay*)
I don't speak French, *je ne parle pas français* (jhuh ne parl pah frahn *say*)
I don't understand, *je ne comprends pas* (jhuh ne kohm *prahn* pas)
I'd like a table, *je voudrais une table* (zhuh voo *dray* ewn tabl)
I'd like to reserve a table, *je voudrais réserver une table* (zhuh voo *dray* rayzehrvay ewn tabl)
for one, *pour un* (poor oon), two, *deux* (duh), *trois* (twah)(3), *quatre* (*kaht*-ruh)(4), *cinq* (sank)(5), *six* (cease)(6), *sept* (set)(7), *huit* (wheat)(8), *neuf* (nerf)(9), *dix* (dease)(10)
waiter/sir, *monsieur* (muh-*syuh*) (never *garçon!*)
waitress/miss, *mademoiselle* (mad mwa *zel*)
knife, *couteau* (koo *toe*)
spoon, *cuillère* (kwee *air*)
fork, *fourchette* (four *shet*)
menu, *la carte* (la cart) (not *menu!*)
wine list, *la carte des vins* (la cart day van)
no smoking, *défense de fumer* (day *fahns* de fu may)
toilets, *les toilettes* (lay twa *lets*)

closed, *fermé* (fehr-may)
open, *ouvert* (oo-vehr)
today, *aujourd'hui* (o zhoor *dwee*)
tomorrow, *demain* (duh *mehn*)

tonight, *ce soir* (suh *swahr*)
Monday, *lundi* (luhn *dee*)
Tuesday, *mardi* (mahr *dee*)
Wednesday, *mercredi* (mair kruh *dee*)
Thursday, *jeudi* (jheu *dee*)
Friday, *vendredi* (vawn druh *dee*)
Saturday, *samedi* (sahm *dee*)
Sunday, *dimanche* (dee *mahnsh*)

here, *ici* (ee-*see*)
there, *là* (la)
what, *quoi* (kwah)
when, *quand* (kahn)
where, *où est* (ooh-eh)
how much, *c'est combien* (say comb bee *ehn*)
credit cards, *les cartes de crédit* (lay kart duh creh *dee*)

Provençal Food & Drink Specialties

aïoli/ailloli, garlic mayonnaise

anchoïade, anchovy spread

banon, cheese dipped in eau-de-vie and wrapped in chestnut leaves

boeuf à la gordienne, braised beef dish

cachat, fresh cheese

cavaillon, a fragrant melon from the town of the same name. It looks like a small cantaloupe

champignon de pin, pine mushroom (a wild mushroom)

daube provençal, gravy with capers, garlic and anchovies

escabèche, raw fish marinated in lime juice and herbs/a cold marinated sardine dish

estouffados, almond butter cookies

farigoule or frigolet, wild thyme

fromage fort, extremely soft cheese mixed with herbs, salt, pepper and marc

herbes de Provence, mixture of herbs that includes fennel, lavender, marjoram, bay leaf, sage, rosemary and thyme

lapin en paquets, rabbit pieces in a packet of bacon

lavande, lavender. Lavender blossoms are added to dishes such as sorbet de lavande (lavender sorbet)

lou maïs, corn-meal cake

marc, a strong liqueur made from distilling the residue of grapes (similar to Italian grappa)

muge, mullet

parme, amberjack

pastis, anise-flavored aperitif. This is a Provençal word meaning mixture. It's a summer drink. Common brands are Pastis 51, Pernod, Ricard, Granier, Prado and Henri Bardouin

petits farcis provençaux, stuffed vegetables

picodon, goat's-milk cheese

pissaladière, pizza-like tart with onions, black olives and purée of anchovies and sardines

provençale, à la, with garlic, onions, herbs and tomatoes ("Provence style")

quartiers d'orange glacés, caramelized orange sections

tapenade, mixture of black olives, olive oil, lemon juice, capers and anchovies (a spread)

tian de Saint-Jacques et légumes provençal, sea scallops on a bed of chopped vegetables

tomates à la provençal, baked tomatoes stuffed with bread
crumbs, garlic and parsley
trouchia, an omelet (in most of France, this means trout)
violet de Provence, braid of garlic
Nice/French Riviera Food & Drink Specialties
bohémienne, eggplant and tomato casserole
daube à la niçoise, beef or lamb stew with red wine, tomatoes
and onions
farci, a dish of stuffed vegetables
lou pevre, goat's-milk cheese with coarsely ground pepper
lou piech, stuffed veal dish
niçoise, usually means with tomatoes, anchovies, vinegar and
black olives
pan bagnat, large round sandwich filled with olive oil, onions,
olives, tomatoes, anchovies and a hard-boiled egg. A specialty
on the Côte d'Azur (means "wet bread"). This is a salade niçoise
sandwich
pissaladière, pizza-like tart with onions, black olives and purée
of anchovies and sardines
ratatouille, eggplant casserole
salade niçoise, salad usually with tomatoes, anchovies or tuna,
potatoes, vinegar and black olives
socca, crêpe made with chickpea flour
stockfish, spicy fish stew

You'll also find such Italian pasta favorites as gnocchi and ravioli on many menus.

7. INDEX

If you're traveling to Provence, check out *Provence Made Easy*
(available in paperback and ebook). A few of the destinations
featured in this handy guide are:
•Avignon •Arles •Nîmes •Marseille
•Aix-en-Provence •Luberon
Available at www.eatndrink.com and www.amazon.com

Printed in Great Britain
by Amazon

84154064R00068